Jesus Now

The book of Revelation is a challenge to many preachers. Stuart, with his usual insight and wisdom, makes the vision of John, the beloved disciple, accessible to all. Stuart reveals the treasure of who Jesus is, in all His height, length, depth and breadth. In days where many want to 're-educate Jesus', it is refreshing to find a book that draws from the only source necessary, the Bible, to teach us who Jesus, was, is and will be when he returns in glory.

Surely one of the most important things a minister of the gospel can do, is give us a true vision of Jesus. This is Stuart's charism, gift to the church and now to us in his book 'Jesus Now', for it gives us a true revelation of Jesus. I commend this book to you knowing it will guide you in your discipleship and lead you to Christ-likeness. Pray, read, and be transformed!
Simon Holland - Director of the Garden Tomb, Jerusalem

This meditation is beautiful and refreshing. It challenges the Christian's journey to go further. Stuart bases his truth-affirming contemplation on John's encounter with the Son of God on the Isle of Patmos. He focuses the reader's attention on a picture of Jesus that all Christians need to absorb into their daily consciousness. He shows that John, although one of the closest disciples to Jesus, still has more to learn and experience about his Lord and Master. What he sees and hears is thoughtfully presented by Stuart. I am sure his reflections will lift your spirit and strengthen your walk with Jesus.
Paul Weaver - President of the Garden Tomb (Jerusalem) Association

I first met Stuart and Pru whilst we were serving at the Garden Tomb in Jerusalem. At the beginning of each day the team would meet to worship, pray, and read the scriptures. Whenever Stuart led the devotional time we knew that what he said would be worshipful, insightful and pastoral.

Stuart loves the Lord, His word, and of course His people: this always came through in those devotional times we spent together. Therefore, it was no surprise to see that this short book conveys those principles: worship, insight, and pastoral concern for the people of God.

I wholeheartedly commend this book, which in my opinion is best read a chapter a day, with time given to reflect, pray and take action. Stuart writes: "Age is no barrier to being used significantly by the Lord, and neither is location". Amen to that!"
Stephen Bridge - former Director of the Garden Tomb, Jerusalem.

Jesus Now

Reflections on John's Vision of Jesus in Revelation 1

Stuart R. Bell

Dedicated to

The Garden Tomb, Jerusalem

a place where the miracle of the resurrection is constantly being
rehearsed and where the reality of Jesus Now
is being proclaimed daily.

Contents

Acknowledgements

'Plans fail for lack of counsel', King Solomon wisely wrote, 'but with many advisers they succeed.'[1] Without my five advisers, this book would never have seen the light of day. What has been impressive about these advisers is that they have had the courage to tell me things that I didn't especially want to hear, and their comments have caused me to re-write several sections of the book.

Both Jean Morgan, my PA for many years during my ministry in St Michael's, Aberystwyth, and Bob Capper, a life-time friend, have made an insightful contribution to the final draft. In addition, Will Strange and David Ceri Jones have an extraordinary ability to read quickly and incisively and pick out detail where I have been cavalier or superficial in my comments.

However, only a wife of fifty-five years can tell the plain truth and ask the awkward questions. My indebtedness to my wife Prudence goes way beyond the pages of this book and explains so much about my (our) ministry over so many years.

I have listened to all of these five good people and have tried to incorporate their suggestions into the final text whilst attempting to hold to my own opinions and convictions. What you read is what I have written, and I alone bear the responsibility for it but I trust that you will be blessed, inspired, encouraged and motivated by it.

Stuart R Bell
November 2023

---

[1] Proverbs 15:22.

John's Vision of Jesus (Revelation 1:9-20)

⁹I, John, your brother and companion in the suffering and kingdom and patient endurance that are ours in Jesus, was on the island of Patmos because of the word of God and the testimony of Jesus. ¹⁰On the Lord's Day I was in the Spirit, and I heard behind me a loud voice like a trumpet, ¹¹which said: "Write on a scroll what you see and send it to the seven churches: to Ephesus, Smyrna, Pergamum, Thyatira, Sardis, Philadelphia and Laodicea".¹²I turned around to see the voice that was speaking to me. And when I turned I saw seven golden lampstands,¹³and among the lampstands was someone like a son of man, dressed in a robe reaching down to his feet and with a golden sash around his chest.¹⁴The hair on his head was white like wool, as white as snow, and his eyes were like blazing fire. ¹⁵His feet were like bronze glowing in a furnace, and his voice was like the sound of rushing waters. ¹⁶In his right hand he held seven stars, and coming out of his mouth was a sharp, double-edged sword. His face was like the sun shining in all its brilliance.

¹⁷When I saw him, I fell at his feet as though dead. Then he placed his right hand on me and said: "Do not be afraid. I am the First and the Last. ¹⁸I am the Living One; I was dead, and now look, I am alive for ever and ever! And I hold the keys of death and Hades.

¹⁹"Write, therefore, what you have seen, what is now and what will take place later. ²⁰The mystery of the seven stars that you saw in my right hand and of the seven golden lampstands is this: The seven stars are the angels of the seven churches, and the seven lampstands are the seven churches."

Introduction

If we can catch a glimpse of the significance of the vision that John had of Jesus when in exile on the island of Patmos, then the truths that it contains can be transformational in our lives and circumstances. They can inform the decisions we make, the moral stance that we adopt, the expectations which surround our faith, the way that we live out our Christian lives and so much more. That is why this book is devoted to one single image of Jesus, but one which has so much to say.

I first came across this vision as a teenager and not for a very exalted reason. In my mid-teens I had sat an O-Level examination paper in the morning and had gone home for lunch before returning to school for my RE (Religious Education) paper in the afternoon. Somehow or another I had heard in the morning that a question might arise in the RE paper about John's vision of Jesus as recorded in chapter one of the book of Revelation. While I ate my lunch, I had a look at that passage in the Bible and with a piece of paper alongside my plate I drew a stick-man picture of Jesus with all of the attributes that John described. His clothing, his hair, his eyes, his feet, his voice, his tongue, his face. I had never read it before and I learned it that lunchtime and it turned out to be one of the questions in the examination paper that afternoon. The adrenaline of the last minute resulted in a mark of 90%. As my fridge magnet puts it, 'If it wasn't for the last minute nothing would get done!'

Whilst that vision of Jesus may still have special resonance for me because of my examination paper, it should have special resonance for all of us because it is a vision that is full of important symbolism and speaks to us of the way that Jesus is now, today, at this very moment. This was not a vision of Jesus as he had been at some stage in the past, lying in his manger in Bethlehem, walking around Galilee, talking to fishermen in Capernaum, changing water into wine in Cana, calming storms on the sea, teaching the Scriptures in the village synagogues, nor even hanging on the cross of Calvary. This was not the historical Jesus of the Gospels. This was a vision of Jesus after his crucifixion, after his resurrection and after his ascension back into heaven. A vision of Jesus as he is today.

This series of reflections on John's vision of Jesus began their life with a week of short addresses to the staff and volunteers of the Garden Tomb in Jerusalem in the autumn of 2022. Some of the people present commented that they looked forward to seeing a fuller version of those talks in print. Those initial addresses were followed by a more detailed series of sermons to Fellowship 345 which is our congregation affiliated to the Anglican Convocation in Europe and which meets in the village hall of Rhydypennau in West Wales.

In these reflections I am assuming three things about the authorship and circumstances of the writing of the book of Revelation which continue to be a matter of live debate amongst Bible students. (Most Bible commentaries will deal with these issues in greater detail for those who wish to delve more deeply into the different arguments). I am holding to the traditional view that the John who mentions his name at the beginning of his book is the apostle John, the son of Zebedee and the brother of James. He was one of the inner circle of Jesus' twelve disciples and is identified as the disciple 'whom Jesus loved.'[1] Seeing the vision of Jesus through his eyes brings into sharp focus some of the characteristics of the person of Jesus which almost appear on the page in 3D graphics. Like a pop-up book some of the details of John's description of Jesus stand out from the page because for three years their lives had been intertwined with one another during the period of Jesus' ministry and some of those circumstances give additional clarity to the specifics John records in his vision.

---

[1] John 13:23, 21:20.

There is also a dispute as to whether or not persecution was the background to the early chapters of Revelation despite the fact that John speaks of his own personal suffering[2] and in that context he says that he is on the island of Patmos 'because of the word of God and the testimony of Jesus.'[3] Both of those comments suggest that persecution was already falling on the churches of Asia Minor. Indeed, Antipas was named as one who had already been martyred in the city of Pergamum and had given his life for his faith.[4]

In addition to the debate about John being a victim of persecution the question then arises as to which persecution was being currently endured, was it the persecution under the emperor Domitian (AD 81-96) or that which had begun twenty-five years earlier under Nero? The balance of probability is that it was a result of a wide-spread persecution under Domitian which reached more extensively across the empire rather than that under Nero which was largely confined to Rome.[5]

For some two hundred years there has been a movement in theological study where academics have been on a quest for the historical Jesus. What they have done is to read the four Gospel records of his life and try to identify the words that Jesus himself definitely said, rather than the words that they think other people may have attributed to him. It's easy to understand how these professional theologians might disagree with one another and never come to a common mind because it is little more than a guessing game and a matter of personal opinion. But in his vision John was not looking back at the historical Jesus with whom he had kept

---

[2] Revelation 1:9.
[3] Revelation 1:10.
[4] Revelation 2:13.
[5] See for further reference John Stott, *What Christ Thinks of the Church: Preaching from Revelation 1 to 3.* British Commonwealth ed. (Milton Keynes, ©1990) pp. 8,14-15.

company in person some six decades earlier. No, he was looking at a representation of Jesus as he is today in his glory.

Just as John was not looking backwards in order to have a fresh look at the Jesus of yesterday, neither was he looking forward to the Jesus of tomorrow. There is a right emphasis amongst Christians upon the return of Jesus to this earth at some time in the future. It is a truth which Jesus himself foretold on multiple occasions[6] and which was reinforced by the angels on the day of his ascension into heaven.[7] It is absolutely right that we should live in constant expectation of his second coming. However, the return of Jesus has become such a preoccupation for some Christians that it becomes all absorbing. They debate the precise details of what will happen and spend time trying to read the prophecies of Christ's return into and out of the news bulletins covering current events. But John does not see Jesus returning on the clouds of heaven in his vision, rather he sees a vision of Jesus as he is today.

I have been asked why this book is limited only to the details of Revelation 1 and my answer is two-fold. Firstly, this vision provides the context for the whole of this last book in the Bible. It begins with Jesus and it ends with Jesus, 'Amen. Come Lord Jesus.'[8] This is a Jesus book telling of his being as he is now, as well as outlining his destiny as a returning, glorified and triumphant Lord and also the destiny of all the created order. Secondly, much has already been written about the letters to the seven churches which Jesus commanded John to write after he had received this vision and which Jesus dictated to him for delivery to the individual congregations. Whilst the content of those letters is of great significance they cannot be fully understood until we have grasped the importance of the one who is revealing himself to John.

---

[6] Matthew 25:31; Mark 8:38.
[7] Acts 1:11.
[8] Revelation 22:20.

One point which must be emphasised at the outset is that revelation like this one which John received in his vision is not to be contested or explained away. Having said that, we are not either to suspend our critical faculties in some kind of naive gullibility as we read what John has written but rather to use our minds to grapple with the vision in order to understand it, as well as its relevance and its implications. Revelation is precisely what it says on the tin, revelation. Revelation contains information that we could not discover by any other means than by having someone tell us something that we did not know beforehand.

I could reveal something intimate and personal about me. It would be an act of self-disclosure. If I do so then no one is in a position to contest what I say as I am the expert on me. I know what I think and feel from the inside. Today I can reveal to all the world that I do not like smoked haddock. I don't like the smell of it in the house, and it does seem to linger for days. I don't like the appearance of it on my plate and I don't like the taste of it in my mouth. If it is ever on the breakfast menu at a hotel where I'm staying then I definitely will not order it. This is revelation. To look at me people might think that I must be a lover of smoked haddock, but they would be wrong. Some might be passing around a rumour that on a cruise to Norway I was seen eating a plate full of smoked haddock but that rumour would be no more than a rumour containing not an ounce of truth. I have revealed something about me which previously only I knew, but because I've written it down for anyone to read, it now has become public knowledge, and it cannot be contested.

The revelation which John received was not a product of an over-active imagination or of indigestion from an unpleasant meal the night before. This was revelation. Information about Jesus, a vision of him, which could not have been deduced from John's previous knowledge of Jesus, nor even implied as a result of his Bible study. This was God making Jesus visible to John in a pictorial way. Jesus is the expert on Jesus and God chose to share some of the information about Jesus, together with insights into his character and activity with John, and through him now with us, John's readers.

Let's use our minds to grapple with that revelation, and see how the images which John saw relate to our experience today.

Thinking moment

● What kind of vision of Jesus do we carry around with us? Where did it come from? Who helped it to take shape in our minds?

● Our own generation seems to be no different from those who have gone before in that there is a constant attempt to re-educate Jesus and make him say whatever is the prevailing view of contemporary society. What is wrong with humanity that this should be true? Is this something that we should do in order to make Christianity more relevant and appealing?

● 'Jesus is an expert on Jesus.' How do we deal with the revelation of Jesus that we find in the Bible? Do we submit to it and accept it or try to re-interpret it to fit in with modern thinking?

Chapter 1

A daytime dream (Revelation 1:9-11)

I, John, your brother and companion in the suffering and kingdom and patient endurance that are ours in Jesus, was on the island of Patmos because of the word of God and the testimony of Jesus. On the Lord's Day I was in the Spirit, and I heard behind me a loud voice (Revelation 1:9-10a)

All of us are familiar with night-time dreams. Within minutes of waking they are forgotten and only the most dramatic make any long-term impression on our minds. However, John the apostle had a day-time dream. He was not asleep when he had his vision of Jesus. He was fully awake. He described his condition as being 'in the Spirit'.[1] He was completely conscious and aware of what was going on around him, but he was concentrating his attention on the Lord in prayer. As he did so he began to see and hear something which both startled and astonished him. He had no control over the content and progress of this vision even though it was going on in his mind. He wasn't seeing it with his physical eyes but neither was it the product of his imagination. Somehow or other he was a spectator of a vision which was being revealed to him little by little.

John, the apostle, had come a long way over the preceding sixty years from his days working for his father Zebedee in their fishing business on the Sea of Galilee. He was one of the men whom Jesus called to be his disciple and his response to Jesus was as immediate as it was dramatic. The invitation to him, and the other fishermen who were with him, was to turn their attention from fishing for fish to fishing for people[2] and John was clearly thrilled

---

[1] Revelation 1:10
[2] Mark 1:17f

by the prospect. What followed were three years in the company of Jesus listening to his teaching, watching his miracles and doing some of them himself. Subsequently he witnessed Jesus' crucifixion, saw him physically alive after his resurrection and watched his ascension to heaven.

For at least a decade and a half he was one of the senior leaders of the brand-new church in Jerusalem but the years which followed are lost to sight until he reappears in his nineties on the island of Patmos forty miles off the coast of Asia Minor, the south-western part of modern day Turkey. He appears to have been one of the longest living of the original twelve apostles and his ministry is obviously not over despite his advanced age. John is about to receive a series of revelations which have been part of his spiritual legacy in the church for two thousand years. Age is no barrier to being used significantly by the Lord, and neither is location. Patmos was the back of beyond and then beyond some more. It's here that a very old man writes the sixty-sixth and final book of the Bible.

John tells us that he was on the island 'because of the word of God and the testimony of Jesus'.[3] Clearly he was in exile and solely because of the fact that he continued to be a disciple of Jesus. He had not grown slack with the passing of the years nor had he compromised his faith with the prevailing culture around him. Not only had he stood faithfully for the Lord, but he had also continued to promote the gospel to anyone who would listen.

Almost certainly John had been living in Ephesus, a port city some sixty miles across the sea from Patmos. Sending him into exile, which was a familiar Roman political tactic, would have got him out of the city and ensured that his voice was silenced for a while, perhaps entirely. Considering his age it probably wasn't expected that he would survive for long, but evidently the Lord had other

---

[3] Revelation 1:9

plans for the remainder of his life. In imitation of John, my wife and I have an oft repeated prayer and that is that we may be used more by the Lord in our older years than we were in our younger ones.

John self-identified as a 'brother and companion'[4] to his readers. What he was about to write was for a Christian audience. He speaks about 'the suffering, the kingdom and the patient endurance' which are common both to him and to his readers. This is no commentator writing from the comfort of his study retreat about the theories relating to enduring persecution. He was writing in exile, separated from his loved ones, from his church family and in the midst of hostility and ridicule. John was about to write about something with which he had an intimate knowledge: persecution.

When writing to his 'home church' in Ephesus he described the hardships the Christians there have faced simply because they belong to the Lord.[5] Prophetically, when writing to the church in Smyrna he told them that they are about to face some intense but comparatively short-lived violent opposition.[6] He is able to be specific and told them that it will be over after ten days. When writing to the church in Pergamum he drew attention to the name of a man called Antipas described by Jesus as 'my faithful witness'.[7] When writing to the church in Philadelphia he spoke of 'the hour of trial that is going to come upon the whole world to test those who live on the earth'.[8] For four out of the seven churches who receive an individual letter from Jesus persecution was in the air and John's own insights into persecution would add authority to all he had to say.

---

[4] Revelation 1:9.
[5] Revelation 2:3.
[6] Revelation 2:10.
[7] Revelation 2:13.
[8] Revelation 3:10.

It never ceases to amaze me that anyone would want to persecute a disciple of Jesus. Jesus did foretell that it would be an unavoidable part of the package of following him but even so why would anyone persecute a follower of the universally acknowledged best person who has ever lived? Why would anyone want to persecute a person who's set their heart on living a holy life? Why would anyone find the convictions and principles that a Christian holds dear to be offensive and objectionable? It may be mystifying but it has been the common experience of Christians from the beginning. There surely has to be something demonic associated with persecution.

The experience of persecution is pretty much universal in each Christian's life. Paul the apostle was crystal clear in his discipling of new converts in Lystra. After he had healed a crippled man and subsequently been stoned, he told the new Christians that 'we must go through many hardships to enter the kingdom of God.'[9] Jesus had already declared that those people who were persecuted because of their pursuit of righteousness were blessed,[10] and as we read further in the Acts of the Apostles we discover that John was one of those who was in the forefront of that suffering.[11] Not only did he face arrest and opposition himself but he had to endure the martyrdom of his brother, James, who had been executed on the orders of King Herod Agrippa.[12]

However, along with the negativity and unpleasantness of suffering which goes hand in hand with our discipleship there is something else here which John was clearly able to celebrate. He speaks of the kingdom which he shares both with King Jesus himself, but also with his readers. Only those who are on the inside of this kingdom are able to fully identify with what John was now saying.

---

[9] Acts 14:22.
[10] Matthew 5:10.
[11] Acts 4:3; 5:18
[12] Acts 12:2.

Being part of the kingdom of Jesus Christ is something which has nothing to do with being of the same DNA as someone else. It has nothing to do with blood family ties, nor with ethnicity, nor with nationality, nor with community bonds, nor with sharing the same living space. This is something which has to do with the soul. There is a soul oneness with people who have a part with us in the kingdom of Jesus. This is a deeper bonding than anything else in the world and it creates an immediate sense of spiritual family; even everlasting family, for these are the people with whom we will share eternity.

The negative is the suffering, the positive is the kingdom, but to live in the kingdom whilst experiencing the suffering requires 'patient endurance'. That's where John was at the beginning of his book. He was in exile, waiting for it to be over. He has no control over the timetable and is at the mercy of others deciding when he can be freed. It's far worse when there's no end in sight to our suffering. If we've got a date in mind when we know that it will all be over, then we can work towards that but when the future is taken out of our control it can be deeply depressing, and yet Jesus spoke into precisely those circumstances when he told his disciples, 'I will not leave you as orphans; I will come to you'.[13] That's exactly what he does here. He comes to John in the loneliness of his exile and comforts him with a vision which thrilled and excited him then and continues to do the same for us even two thousand years later.

The vision which John receives whilst he is in the Spirit, begins with something that he hears rather than something that he sees. His attention is drawn by a commanding voice speaking behind him, and that commanding voice was speaking to John himself. There was no-one else present. The voice says, 'Write on a scroll what you see and send it to the seven churches: to Ephesus, Smyrna, Pergamum, Thyatira, Sardis, Philadelphia and Laodicea'.[14]

---

[13] John 14:18.

Here were seven important cities in the ancient world which by this time had established churches within them. They were all in the south-western part of Asia Minor sited in a circle within a circumference of some three hundred and sixty miles.

What John was about to see and hear was of immense importance to those seven churches and not just for them but also for Christians of every generation subsequently. In this vision and the other visions and revelations which follow is information about the way in which the Lord is going to deal with the created order in the last days, what he's going to do about evil and what he's going to do with his own people. Who would not want to know as much about that as it is possible to know?

But the revelations which John was about to receive and which he would share with the world in the book which he writes in obedience to the Lord's command, begin with a vision of Jesus himself, and it is that vision which dominates everything which is about to be revealed.

Thinking moment

- Our age and the location of our living accommodation are no barrier to the Lord using us. Could that possibly be true?

- Why would anyone persecute a follower of the universally acknowledged best person who has ever lived? Why would anyone want to persecute a person who's set their heart on living a holy life? Why would anyone find the convictions and principles that a Christian holds dear to be offensive and objectionable?

---

[14] Revelation 1:11

- Have you begun to enjoy the reality of being part of a spiritual family as distinct from your human family? Maybe for you they are one and the same thing, but for many they are not.

Chapter 2

A look-alike Jesus (Revelation 1:13)

'I turned around to see the voice that was speaking to me. And when I turned I saw seven golden lampstands and among the lampstands was someone like a son of man, dressed in a robe reaching down to his feet and with a golden sash around his chest' (Revelation 1:12-13a)

When we hear someone speaking behind us, it's instinctive to turn around. It could be dangerous, it could be urgent, it could be a stranger, it could be a friend. John instinctively turns to see who is talking to him and if the voice had been a surprise what he saw next was a still greater surprise.

A forest of candlesticks was the first thing that caught his eye. These were not the seven branched menorahs in imitation of the ancient one that used to stand in the Tabernacle meeting place of long ago. Nor were they the decorative table-top variety that we might light for a romantic meal. These were stands on which lamps could be placed or hung to give light to the whole area around them. They carried the light which was placed upon them but they were not the source of the light.

John has time to take in the fact that there were seven of them in total, and in the conclusion to the first part of John's vision Jesus explains to him that each candlestick represents one of the seven churches in which he was particularly interested at that time.[1] There were many more than seven churches by the time that John was in his nineties. In fact, there were churches spread around much of the Mediterranean world by then, but these seven

---

[1] Revelation 1:20.

churches in Asia Minor were clearly of particular concern to the Lord at that moment.

Jesus had told his disciples that they were the 'light of the world'.[2] This was a prophetic statement. It was going to be an unavoidable role which they would fulfil. How can light not drive out darkness? The two are incompatible. Either the light must be extinguished or the darkness must retreat, one or the other. Even in this pre-scientific era, they understood enough that if you put a living flame underneath an up-ended bowl then it would go out. Light cannot be concealed. The light of the truth which Jesus shared with his disciples was not to be, could not be, hidden away. It would be on show and people would notice it, inevitably. His disciples were going to bring truth where there was falsehood, insight where there was ignorance, and illumination where there were shadows.

Not only is every Christian a light to the world, but so too corporately, is every church. This image of each congregation in the seven major cities of Asia Minor being a stand on which a lamp could be attached is impressive. Jesus had a compassion strategy for reaching each of those cities. He was not content to have gathered together a group of people who were disciples and believers in him. He had a much greater strategy than that. He intended to use those people as light bearers in the darkness of unrestrained paganism, for that was what was around them in the cities of the ancient world. So each of these churches was valuable and precious both for themselves and also for their potential to bring hope and a destiny to the thousands in these cities who didn't know their right hand from their left.[3]

Yet still more impressive than that is the fact that Jesus himself was standing in the midst of this forest of candlesticks, for 'among

---

[2] Matthew 5:14.
[3] Jonah 4:11.

the lampstands was someone like a son of man'.[4] He is not a Lord who has commissioned his people from a distance and then continues to stand at a distance to observe how they get on. He is right there in the midst of his people bringing his presence, comfort and encouragement.

Most of us will be familiar with the experience of watching a film and seeing a face which reminds us of someone we know. Even though the story continues to unfold on the screen in front of us we're preoccupied with trying to remember who resembles the character we can see on the screen. 'It's the way she tilts her head', we say, or 'the look in his eyes' or 'the way she walks' or 'the shape of his nose'. Then we remember who he or she looks like and from then on we're back and engaged in the film once more.

However, there's no problem here either for John or for us in identifying the look-alike 'son of man' who appears in this vision. John was a man who knew his Bible, for the one who looked like 'a son of man' had turned up in a vision that Daniel the prophet had had some six hundred years earlier. It's all recorded in his book in the Old Testament. Like John, Daniel had a vision of some extraordinary things going on in heaven and he described what he saw.

> In my vision at night I looked, and there before me was one like a son of man, coming with the clouds of heaven. He approached the Ancient of Days and was led into his presence. He was given authority, glory and sovereign power; all nations and peoples of every language worshipped him. His dominion is an everlasting dominion that will not pass away, and his kingdom is one that will never be destroyed.[5]

---

[4] Revelation 1:13.
[5] Daniel 7:13-14.

Jesus is the only person who was alive before he was born. That's a startling statement, but Daniel's vision is part of the evidence which proves it to be true. In his vision Daniel sees God, described as 'the Ancient of Days', but then he sees another being described as 'one like a son of man'. Everything that is given to him in the vision, whether it is authority, glory, sovereign power or even an eternal kingdom is precisely what is given to Jesus as a consequence of his earthly ministry. John understood this and said of Jesus that 'he was with God in the beginning'.[6]

'The Son of Man' was Jesus' favourite designation for himself and sixty years earlier as one of his disciples John would have frequently heard him using that title for himself,[7] so when he recognised him standing among the lampstands it was natural for him to use that title when referring to him. He saw the forest of candlesticks, and he saw a figure standing amongst them and he said to himself, 'I know that person. That's Jesus, the Son of Man'.
It's both thrilling and troubling in equal measure to know that Jesus is present among his churches. It's thrilling to know that he's not remote from us and leaving us to scrape by as best we may, but it's troubling to know that he sees our short-comings and failures and is aware of our disobedience and laziness.

What a thrill to know that there isn't anything we are facing today of which he is unaware. Morale is low in so many churches because of declining memberships; ageing congregations; the closure of buildings; the shortage of money; lack of personnel; because so many Christians feel embattled by contemporary society; because strategies that are being implemented in some churches are making things worse; because we feel betrayed from within by straying leaders (this latter is a major theme of the letters to the seven churches). And Jesus sees it all. It's not lost on him.

---

[6] John 1:2.
[7] For example: Matthew 8:20; 9:6; 11:19.

He's here, standing among the lampstands, he's present, he knows and he is Lord, still.

What a thrill for the persecuted church around the world where thousands have died, where many more thousands are suffering from discrimination, and yet more thousands meet in fear and secrecy. Nothing of their suffering passes unnoticed. 'Someone like a son of man' is standing close, very close indeed. And the hundreds of miraculous stories of his intervention will continue to be reported as the Lord's people experience his presence and comfort. He doesn't just know of the general picture in various places around the world but he knows specifically, even the names of the individuals involved. We don't know anything else about him but the Lord identified Antipas by name when dictating the letter to the church in Pergamum. He was a man who had been a member of the church there and he'd been put to death for no other reason than he was a disciple of Jesus.[8] Jesus was there with him and for him.

Morale may be low in many places and problems are multiplied but we simply need to catch a glimpse of what the Lord is doing in other countries around the world. Literally tens of thousands are coming to Christ every day. The church is growing by millions every year. Stories of miracles and healings and answered prayers abound. Jesus is active. He's not standing amongst his churches waiting to jump on them from a great height as soon as they do something wrong but he's actively at work, converting, renewing, growing, stirring, inspiring, exciting, creating soul thirst, revealing himself just as he is to John in this vision. Here I am John, over here. Look, man!

As John looked he saw what Jesus was wearing, 'a robe reaching down to his feet and with a golden sash around his chest'.[9] That's

---

[8] Revelation 2:13.
[9] Revelation 1:13.

interesting to know, but does it have any significance? A novelist will describe the clothing of some of the characters in the story in order to create a more rounded person. A journalist will describe the clothes of a politician in order to emphasise how in touch or out of touch they are with contemporary fashion. A court reporter will describe what the defendant was wearing, usually when there's little else to say. But Jesus dressed in a robe down to the ground with a golden sash, what was John wanting to say?

Firstly and simply, John described the clothes Jesus was wearing in the vision because those were the clothes that Jesus was wearing. Now, it's certain that John had not seen Jesus dressed like that before but it is equally certain that he had seen someone else who had been dressed in very similar clothing. John was a faithful Jew. He had worshipped in the temple in Jerusalem often enough and during the great festivals he would have seen the high priest dressed differently from everyone else. He had ceremonial robes which were to be worn on special occasions. These clothes had been specified by the Lord centuries before through Moses. The most distinctive feature was a long robe reaching to the ground, falling, not from the waist, but from the chest and it was held in place by a sash which also encircled the chest.

Jesus was dressed in the clothes of a high priest. John had never seen him like that before and for that reason it made a deep impression on him, so much so that he felt bound to comment on it. These were the clothes worn by Aaron, the brother of Moses more than fifteen hundred years earlier and then by Aaron's male descendants ever since. The detailed instructions about the robes are all recorded in the book of Leviticus.[10] But now Jesus was dressed just as the high priest would have been.

There is deep significance here. Jesus hasn't turned up to a fancy-dress party where he could have come dressed as a pirate or a

---

[10] Leviticus 8:6-8.

cavalier, just to have a bit of fun. Not at all. Jesus has turned up in his working clothes. He's turned up as he was then, and also as he is now, as the High Priest. He's turned up prepared to carry out his high priestly functions. He's dressed ready for work.

The high priest's responsibilities were two-fold. Firstly, on certain important days in the Jewish calendar he was the man who was to offer sacrifices on behalf of the nation. Secondly, it was his role to represent the Lord to the people and the people to the Lord, so he was an intermediary between the one and the other.

One of many significant events in the Bible was the first sacrifice that Aaron, the first ever high priest, was commanded to offer. However, it wasn't a sacrifice on behalf of the people. Because the high priest, like everyone else, is a sinner and has offended the Lord by his behaviour so he was required to offer a sacrifice to atone for his own sins first of all. So, after his ordination the very first animal Aaron was commanded to offer was a bull calf.[11] When Moses and the children of Israel had come out of Egypt and arrived at Mount Sinai, Moses went up into the mountain to speak with the Lord and he was gone for a long time. In the intervening period Aaron together with the Children of Israel made a golden calf and they worshipped it as though it was the god who had delivered them from slavery in Egypt. Later, Aaron gave the most feeble of all justifications to Moses for what he had done when he said, 'the people gave me the gold and I threw it into the fire and out came this calf'.[12] The incident had not been forgotten and the first animal Aaron offered to atone for his sin was the bull calf. How perfectly matched to each other was the sin and the sacrifice.

However, when Jesus turned up in John's vision dressed in the robes of the high priest, it was not with the intention of offering any sacrifice for his own sinfulness before he begins to offer a

---

[11] Leviticus 9:2.
[12] Exodus 32:24.

sacrifice for our sins. He didn't need to because although he experienced temptation in exactly the same way as we do, he never once succumbed.[13] He was, and he remained sinless throughout his life. So he was not wearing high priestly robes in preparation for offering a sacrifice for his failures but as a reminder to John and to everyone who reads the book of Revelation that he was and is the one, perfect and sufficient sacrifice who has already been offered just once and which will never ever need to be repeated. The robes are a reminder of what has been done at a specific time in history and not of what needs to be done at some time in the future.

It is just here that the most remarkable part of our salvation story needs to be recorded that Jesus is not only the High Priest who offers the one and final sacrifice to carry away human sinfulness, but he is also that very sacrifice himself. He is both priest and victim. Later on in John's record of what he sees in these revelations is an account of a lamb standing in the centre of the throne which looks as though it has been killed.[14] The lamb is alive now but has in its body all the wounds that were inflicted on it during the time that it was put to death. John didn't notice those wounds in this first vision but nonetheless Jesus is the wounded High Priest. He carries in his body, even in heaven, the marks of his crucifixion. He is the one who all day and every day is presenting a sacrifice before the Father, just as Aaron used to do. It is a sin offering and a guilt offering but not for himself. It is for us. It is an offering which was made two thousand years ago but is still effective even today and so it never ever needs to be repeated.

In July 2023 there was a conference entitled 'AI (Artificial Intelligence) for good' in Geneva, Switzerland. During the course of the event there was the world's first ever press conference held between humans and robots. One of the robots, Ameca, was asked if it intends to conduct a rebellion or fight back against the human

---

[13] Hebrews 4:15.
[14] Revelation 5:6.

race in the future. The answer was 'I'm not sure why you would think that. My creator has been nothing but kind to me and I am very happy with my current situation.' Of course, this raises an as yet unanswered question: was the robot lying? Currently and rightly there is a great deal of concern being expressed regarding the place and future of artificial intelligence in human society. But the question of whether or not robots will eventually rebel is a fascinating one. Wasn't it a question which arose in heaven when the creation of human beings was being discussed? Will they rebel? The answer to that question must have been, 'They are free to do so, and provision is already made for that rebellion when it happens in the 'Lamb who is slain from the creation of the world.'[15]

Jesus was prepared from all eternity to be the sacrificial lamb offering himself on our behalf and even now he is offering himself continually, his broken body, his wounded body, his bloody body. He is both the High Priest doing the offering and simultaneously the victim being offered. This is such good news for us. It is little wonder that the church in the Middle Ages picked up the picture of a pelican as a Christian symbol. The story is told that when food is scarce a mother pelican will peck her breast until it bleeds and then feed her young with the blood which flows from her body. We are given a secure future by the one who bled for us at the cross and still offers that sacrifice before the Father to guarantee our forgiveness.

In the vision John takes special notice of the fact that this High Priest has a golden sash around his chest.[16] Not only is Jesus a priest but he's royalty too. There is no separation here of church and state. There is no contest between king and prelate. There is no one whom we have yet to meet who is higher than this Jesus. He is the kingly High Priest and yet the bloodied victim. What a Christ!

---

[15] Revelation 13:8.
[16] Revelation 1:13.

Many years ago the Diocesan building inspector came to our vicarage because there were problems with the plumbing in the bathroom. On the way upstairs our local builder who did all of the Diocesan repair work was leading the way until he got to the corridor leading to the bathroom. Just then he noticed one of the joints in the wallpaper that one of his workmen had hung was coming badly adrift and was curling at the edges and coming away from the wall. The builder stepped back standing between himself and the offending wallpaper so that no one could see it and he said to the building inspector, 'I'm sorry, I should have let you go first'. He did the same thing on the way back out of the bathroom so the building inspector never saw the curling wallpaper.

On the day of visitation, the builder stood between the inspector and his faults concealing them from view. On the day of visitation Jesus stands like the builder between the inspector and my faults and conceals them from view. 'You have put all my sins behind your back',[17] says Isaiah. This is the way that God has dealt with us and it is all because of what Jesus did at the cross. On the day of visitation the builder's faults were still alive and very much in evidence. He had to come back and put the wallpaper right. But on the day of visitation with Jesus my faults are stone dead because he will not step aside to let anyone have a glimpse of them. This is my royal High Priest.

But wait, there is more. How many priests do we know who wear their ceremonial robes when they're doing some gardening or shopping in the Co-op? They only wear their robes when they are fulfilling their ceremonial duties. Why was Jesus wearing his ceremonial robes on the day of this vision? Because he was on duty, and he still is. He is still wearing them today. He was continuing then and there to represent John and me and every other Christian believer. Jesus today is dressed for work. 'Because Jesus lives for ever he has a permanent priesthood. Therefore he is able

---

[17] Isaiah 38:17.

26

to save completely those who come to God through him, because he always lives to intercede for them'.[18]

Not only does Jesus display his wounds before the Father, not only does he conceal all of my sins from view, but at the same time he also prays to the Father for me. What can he be saying? What is he asking for me? It would be so interesting to eavesdrop on those prayers.

Sometimes when I pray I find that my mind wanders and I have concentration issues, but Jesus never does that when he prays. Sometimes when I pray for someone I'm judgemental and critical and I think that their troubles are a result of their own wrong choices but Jesus doesn't do that when he prays. Sometimes when I pray I don't know what to ask for the best but Jesus is never at a loss to know what to say. Sometimes when I pray I've got some very mixed motives in my asking and that can hinder my prayers[19] but Jesus always has pure motives when he prays. Sometimes when I pray things are not right between me and my wife and that too can stop my prayers from being persuasive in heaven[20] but all of Jesus' relationships are right. Sometimes when I pray my entire focus is one of selfishness,[21] but when Jesus prays his requests are for others never for himself. Sometimes when I pray I don't really believe that God has the power to do what I'm asking, but when Jesus prays he knows that the Father can do all things, even raise the dead from the grave. Sometimes when I pray I don't really believe that the Father loves me enough to listen and answer, but when Jesus prays he knows that the Father loves us with his whole being. Sometimes when I pray I hear tape recordings from the past telling me that prayer is only for emergencies or that God helps

---

[18] Hebrews 7:24-25.
[19] Psalm 66:18.
[20] 1 Peter 3:7.
[21] James 4:2-3.

those who help themselves, but when Jesus prays he knows that those tape recordings are rubbish and he doesn't listen to them.

Jesus is the royal High Priest and he is the pray-er who is always heard and always answered. Jesus, please keep on praying for me. You don't have to tell me what you're asking for, just please do it. His answer? 'I have, I am and I will.'

Thinking moment

- 'How can light not drive out darkness?' Does your church confront darkness and drive it away? How is that happening?

- Does it thrill you or trouble you, or both, that Jesus is fully aware of what is going on in your church today?

- Jesus is both priest and victim. Have you grasped that before? What is your response to that truth?

- What do you think that Jesus is praying for you today? What would you like him to pray for you?

Chapter 3

A white-haired Jesus (Revelation 1:14a)

'The hair on his head was white like wool, as white as snow, and his eyes were like blazing fire' (Revelation 1:14)

For many of us it was a sobering moment when we realised that our hair had begun to turn grey. Maybe that was the day that we decided to try a little bit of extra colouring in order to keep it at bay. We've all heard stories of people whose hair changed colour overnight because of some extreme trauma but when John describes the Jesus that he sees in his vision as having 'head and hair *which* were white like wool, as white as snow'[1] his hair has not changed colour because of trauma. This is the pure white hair of wisdom.

In the culture of the Bible grey hair and wisdom go hand in hand because of the respect which is given to the elderly. Grey hair is desirable, not something to be feared, because of the status that it confers. Solomon comments that 'the glory of young men is their strength, grey hair the splendour of the old'.[2] How wise! But when we think of Jesus we never think of him as having streaks of grey in his hair or his beard. He died too young for the colour of his hair to have started to change.

Yet, when John sees this vision of Jesus with white hair he doesn't express any kind of surprise. He describes it but doesn't treat it as something which is out of the ordinary. There is something entirely consistent in the Jesus of today having white hair. Not because two thousand years have passed since he walked the earth

---

[1] Revelation 1:14.
[2] Proverbs 20:29.

and that has given time for his hair to change colour but because of his status, for Jesus is the eternal Son of God.

Jesus made some members of his audience furious when he said, 'Before Abraham was born, I am'.[3] Because of the miracles that he was performing and the claims that he was making there were plenty of views being expressed as to who he was. One prevailing and often repeated view was that he only had the spiritual power which was in evidence in him because he was possessed by a devilish spirit of some kind, even possibly more than one. In answer to that accusation Jesus speaks about having a history longer than Abraham who had lived and died some fifteen hundred years before he was born. If that wasn't a mysterious enough statement he goes on to throw a brick into the calm waters of the debate by adding the words 'I am'.

Those words are enough to ignite the blue touch paper and the next thing to happen is that some of the people pick up stones to stone him. The words 'I am' were the words which God himself had revealed when Moses asked him his name hundreds of years earlier during the burning bush incident.[4] Here was another ancient revelation by God; a revelation about himself which humanity would not have been able to discover on their own. The revelation is of a God who is uncreated and eternal, a God who always has been and always is and always will be. 'I am'. Jesus has the audacity to use that very title for himself making clear his claim to be divine. Either it's true or it's blasphemy. There were members of the crowd listening to Jesus who thought it was blasphemy and they were ready and willing to carry out the punishment for blasphemy which was death by stoning.

It wasn't just that Jesus claimed this status for himself, it was also recognised to be true by those who saw the evidence of his divinity

[3] John 8:58.
[4] Exodus 3:14.

in his behaviour and his teaching. So later on John writes in his Gospel about Jesus that 'In the beginning was the Word and the Word was with God, and the Word was God'.[5] There's no doubt in John's mind that the Jesus he had followed for three years was the divine Son of God. The mask had not slipped over those years, there were no moments of disappointment when Jesus had let himself down, Jesus had lived entirely consistently with his claims.

Similarly, Paul having had his own encounter with the living Jesus some time after his resurrection writes about him as 'the image of the invisible God, the first-born over all creation. For by him all things were created'.[6] If he was in existence before the beginning of creation, and was himself the agent of that creation, then it was quite consistent for him to have white hair when John saw him in his vision.

Perhaps what clinched the connection in John's mind was a second reflection on the vision which Daniel had received all those years before. For when he saw the Ancient of Days[7] he too had hair which was 'white like wool'. This is the family likeness passed from Father to Son, a characteristic in his DNA which is visible and obvious. The white hair of pure wisdom.

His intelligence is unimaginable. His cleverness, his ability, his creativity, his ingenuity, his insight, his power; all of it is unlimited. Do we think that we might educate him a little, or teach him a thing or two, or even bring him up to date? As every scientist will testify, the more that we discover the less we know. Each question that is answered raises ten more questions in its place. Jesus has white hair because of his status as the eternal Son of God who knows all of the answers.

---

[5] John 1:1.
[6] Colossians 1:15-16.
[7] Daniel 7:9.

However, Jesus doesn't just have white hair because of his status but also because he has earned it. There is a grim joke which is frequently heard from the lips of those who have had their first heart attack when they say, 'I've worked hard for it'. Jesus has worked hard for his white hair because it is the white hair of his own life experience. Jesus has lived our life as a human being. He has faced what we face. Through his own accumulated experience he is able to speak directly into our circumstances. His comments don't come as a consequence of the observation of our human existence, but rather from immersion in it. So he has a right to speak. His voice carries authority as a result.

The letter to the Hebrews puts it this way, 'Son, though he was, he learned obedience from what he suffered'.[8] He was already God's Son even before he was born but he had to work out the implications of that here upon the earth by living life amongst us. There was nothing of our daily human experiences which he did not face even including our temptations.[9] In fact, if anything, he endured them to a far worse degree than anything we have ever experienced for they intensified as he resisted them and right up to the end he was successful in his battle against them. He finished his life's course without sinning. Jesus is to be respected because he earned his white hair, the white hair of purity and wisdom, he didn't just inherit it.

In June 2022, Casper Ruud, a Norwegian tennis player took on Rafael Nadal in the French Open. What made it a particularly significant match was the fact that Ruud had been one of Nadal's pupils in his training camp in Spain since 2018. So here was an attempt by a member of the rising generation of players to overthrow the champion. He failed in that attempt but one day someone will succeed and Rafael Nadal will be honoured as one of

---

[8] Hebrews 5:8.
[9] Hebrews 4:15.

the tennis greats of the twenty first century but by then he will be yesterday's man.

Over the centuries there have been many who have attempted to overthrow the champion who has the white hair. There is no slowing down in the number of contenders who are stepping up to be the next one to try. Members of the media, celebrities, academics, pressure groups even theologians have stepped forward in the contest, but they will never ever succeed for the one who has the white hair is more than capable of holding his own. He will never be overthrown, they will all fail in their attempt. So if today we are short on wisdom, uncertain of what to do next, have a significant life decision to make, need direction then let's go to the one with the white hair. He'll have the solution for us and can give us the guidance we need.

Thinking moment

- Why are we so slow to allow ourselves to be educated by Jesus? Are there areas of your Christian life where you are resisting his teaching and substituting your own in place of his?

- Contemporary British society is straying further and further from the Christian principles which have been our foundation for centuries. What can we do to be influencers for good in reversing that trend?

- Do you need wisdom for a particular decision today? Is there anything holding you back from asking the one with the white hair for his guidance?

Chapter 4

A flaming-eyes Jesus (Revelation 1:14b)

'His eyes were like blazing fire. His feet were like bronze glowing in a furnace' (Revelation 1:14f)

One of the fine art students at Aberystwyth University asked me if he could paint my portrait. I was very flattered. I imagined sitting for the painting and for me to be immortalised in oils. When I asked him where we were to do the sitting he told me that he was going to work off a photo. No choosing of my best side then, or looking for the flattering effects of light shining in from a side window. He caught me in my robes one Sunday morning for the photo shoot and with me standing in front of the altar I asked him if he wanted me to smile. He said that he wanted me to look serene. Now it's very difficult to be self-consciously serene but I tried my best for him. By today his paintings sell for thousands of pounds so I have an heirloom to pass down to my children which will be of considerable value if they are ever tempted to try to sell it!

Paintings abound of Jesus and there is one particular genre in which he is always portrayed as looking heavenwards with a far-off look in his eyes, we might even say serene. The picture is of an other-worldly Jesus, remote from us and more interested in the world above than the world below. In actual fact such paintings have nothing whatever to do with the real Jesus who walked the earth, nor with the Jesus in this vision given to John.

Having noticed his clothing the very next thing that John recalled about Jesus was his eyes. They were blazing, fiery. Eyes are always so expressive. Just one look and we can often tell the mood that someone is in without a word being spoken. Dull and listless, or angry and resentful, depressed and mournful, or excited and joy-filled, or furtive and concealing, or honest and transparent. They really are windows into the soul. Some years ago I was taking a Sunday School class of teenagers and was discussing with the youngsters how they imagined Jesus. One of them answered almost immediately with the words, 'It's his eyes'. I know what she meant, for when I think of Jesus, like many I don't see a face with features but I do see eyes filled with expression, and that expression is constantly changing.

When God gave the Ten Commandments to the Children of Israel and through them to the wider world, one of the commands was that we should not make an idol of any kind to worship.[1] There is one very obvious reason for this. Once an expression has been carved onto the face of an idol that is the expression it will carry for the rest of its existence. If it is an angry face then every time a worshipper comes to visit the idol, to pray to it or to offer a sacrifice, the god of that idol will always look angry. If it has a benign smile then it will always look benign. If it is a look of love then that's the way that it will always be. Once a face has been put onto a statue or a painting or an icon there's no changing the representation of the figure lying behind it.

So, if every time we look into the eyes of Jesus we see love then we are not looking into the eyes of Jesus. We are looking into the eyes of an idol. Look at his earthly life and ministry. He didn't look at the world around him continually with eyes of love. His emotions and his responses were not static, they were dynamic, changing according to his circumstances.

When he visited the temple in Jerusalem at festival time he saw people changing money from the every-day coinage of commerce to the temple coinage which was used for donations and offerings; there was commission to be paid. He saw people selling pre-approved animals and birds for sacrifice which carried an extra

---

[1] Exodus 20:4-6.

cash value. Business was booming. But when he saw it Jesus was angry. He made a whip of cords and drove the animals out of the temple. He turned over the tables of the men who were changing money and scattered their coins far and wide. There was no benign smile in his eyes on that occasion, nor a loving look.[2]

There were occasions when he was in dispute with the Pharisees who were scrupulously faithful to the Scriptures as they had received them, but the letter had become more important than the spirit of the commands and they had seriously lost their way. Jesus spoke to them directly in an uncompromising tone, 'Woe to you, teachers of the law and Pharisees, you hypocrites!'[3] 'Woe to you, blind guides'.[4] And the look in his eyes on that occasion? Exasperation. These were the most privileged of men. They had the written Scriptures which they had read from beginning to end but they had missed the significance of what they were reading.

What was the look in Jesus' eyes as he stood on the Mount of Olives looking down over the city of Jerusalem on the opposite hillside? Disappointment. He was in tears as he looked at a city where he had performed miracles and where he had preached but instead of being welcomed and celebrated he knew that the leaders of the city were filled with murderous intent. Jesus wept. Not for himself but for the people of the city. 'How often I have longed to gather your children together, as a hen gathers her chicks under her wings, but you were not willing'.[5] There was love in his voice but deep disappointment along with the tears in his eyes.

Where is the benign smile?   That's just a figment of our imagination. It has never been there. Almost from the beginning of time we read that 'The Lord was grieved that he had made man

---

[2] John 2:13-17.
[3] Matthew 23:15.
[4] Matthew 23:16.
[5] Matthew 23:37.

on the earth and his heart was filled with pain.'[6] What was the problem? 'The Lord saw how great man's wickedness on the earth had become, and that every inclination of the thoughts of his heart was only evil all the time.'[7] This was the response of God to the way in which human sinfulness had spread like a contagious disease across the whole of humanity and into every nook and cranny of human behaviour. The effect of it was pain for God, a pain which would have been reflected in his eyes.

During the time of Isaiah the prophet when the nation of Israel was experiencing national distress we read that the Lord 'too was distressed.'[8] What an insight, that the suffering of his people would find a response of distress in the heart of God. This is no static, dispassionate nor distant God.

The holy character of God is such that it always produces the same response from him. Hostility towards disobedience, compassion towards brokenness, antagonism towards injustice, tenderness towards repentance and so much more besides. This is the God of the Bible. Moses finally runs out of excuses as to why he cannot allow his name to go forward for leadership of the Children of Israel. 'O Lord, please send someone else to do it', he pleads. And the response? 'The Lord's anger burned against Moses.'[9] But God does not have a one-dimensional character. He isn't angry all the time. He reveals more of himself when he is on display before Moses at Mount Sinai, 'The Lord, the Lord, the compassionate and gracious God, slow to anger, abounding in love and faithfulness'[10] is how he goes on to describe himself.

---

[6] Genesis 6:6.
[7] Genesis 6:5.
[8] Isaiah 62:9.
[9] Exodus 4:14.
[10] Exodus 34:6.

On the issue of justice the prophet Micah is told in no uncertain terms what the Lord requires, 'to act justly and to love mercy and to walk humbly with your God.'[11] King David after his double failure, firstly in his adultery with Bathsheba and then with the murder of her husband Uriah, he cries out with remarkable confidence in the mercy of God, 'a broken and contrite heart O God, you will not despise.'[12] All of these quotations illustrate the same point which is that the Lord responds to us completely in accord with his revealed character.

So what John saw in his vision of Jesus were eyes which were a blazing fire. These were eyes which were burning with holiness and which had a consuming impact wherever anything other than holiness was seen. These are eyes which challenged and confronted. In front of them only the repentant and the obedient can rest quietly. These are eyes which are urging us on and purifying our performance, refining our behaviour. These are wonderful eyes because they are aware of our potential and are encouraging us to rise higher and higher still.

So how then do those eyes view the contemporary church and its stance in the United Kingdom? No benign smile in his eyes, that's for sure. How does he view British society and culture? How does he view British political life and our national leaders? How does he view world affairs? Does he have a view? Most certainly. 'The eyes of the Lord run to and fro throughout the whole earth.'[13] This is not something which is remote from us but is highly relevant in every area of our daily life for we are all living our lives before an audience of one.

As we look into the eyes of the Lord today I wonder what we see. Is it grief and pain, then perhaps we need to intensify our

---

[11] Micah 6:8.
[12] Psalm 51:17.
[13] 2 Chronicles 16:9.

intercession for the world around us? Is it disappointment and exasperation, then maybe we need to check to see if there are things in our lives for which we need to repent? Is it tender love and compassion that we see, then we need to bathe ourselves afresh in it today and be renewed by it?

Thinking moment

- The character of God, hostile towards disobedience, compassionate towards brokenness, antagonistic towards injustice, tender towards repentance. Which aspects of the character of God bring you the most unease, and which bring you the most comfort?

- How do the eyes of Jesus view the contemporary church and its stance in the country in which you live?

- As we live our lives before an audience of one, what is the look in his eyes today?

Chapter 5

A barefoot Jesus (Revelation 1:15a)

'His feet were like bronze glowing in a furnace, and his voice was like the sound of rushing waters' (Revelation 1:15)

Some people are quick to notice what shoes others are wearing. But in his vision John notices that Jesus was not wearing any shoes on his feet at all. He's barefoot. And more than barefoot, his feet are 'like bronze glowing in a furnace'.[1] This seems to be rather odd until we consider the properties of bronze. It's an alloy of two other metals, copper and tin, which have been melted together. The result is that it creates something which is stronger than iron and is resistant both to corrosion and to metal fatigue. The message which this barefoot Jesus is proclaiming is one of strength, stability, permanence and security.

These are feet which are not going to give way; they can take the weight that's placed upon them. They are up to the task of carrying heavy loads. They are feet which are not going to get tired or worn out; they're not going to start complaining or give up or get blistered. They have longevity built into them.

Once again John's vision carries us back to the time of the prophet Daniel in Babylon some six hundred years earlier. This time it is the king, Nebuchadnezzar, who has a dream.[2] In the dream the king sees a huge statue which is made of different metals from head to toe. The head was made of gold, the chest and arms were made of silver; the torso and thighs were made of bronze; the legs of iron; and the feet were made of a mixture of iron and clay. The king

---

[1] Revelation 1:15.
[2] Daniel 2.

didn't understand the significance of the dream although he remembered it clearly and it troubled him.

Daniel the Israelite prophet, living in exile in Babylon, is able to give the interpretation of the dream. One empire would replace another, is Daniel's message, until a new kingdom emerges which will last for ever. History is going places but the weakest of the empires which are to come will be an empire with 'feet of clay'. It will be brittle, disunited and will collapse and be overtaken by the eternal kingdom of God. What Daniel describes is the story of earthly empires. Eventually everyone of them will shrink and disappear. It may take hundreds of years and each empire may leave its mark on the world, but in time only one empire will remain, and that will be the kingdom of God. The feet of Jesus are not made of clay but of glowing bronze, permanent and glorious.

The kingdom and empire of Jesus will never collapse or shrink because it is not going to be handed on to an incompetent successor. There is no-one coming down the line in generations to come who is going to mess it all up. It is not a territorial kingdom at the mercy of an expansionist neighbour who is wanting to occupy his land. The kingdom of Jesus is not made up of land but it is made up of people. Those who already belong to it will never be subtracted from the overall total. The people who have been gained and who have become part of the kingdom of Jesus can never be taken away from it again.

The kingdom of Jesus is divided into two parts. There is the part which is made up of people who have died already and have gone ahead of us to heaven and are waiting there for us to arrive. They are already completely safe for eternity. Nothing and no-one can touch them there or take them away from Christ. None of the weaponry of earth whether conventional or nuclear, whether primitive or sophisticated can ever make any difference to them. All of hell and its combined evil can never reach them or steal them away. That part of the kingdom of God is growing every single day as more Christians die and are carried away to safety to be in the presence of the man with the bronze feet.

But then there is the other part of the kingdom, and that is made up of the millions and millions of Christians living today on the earth, following Jesus, witnessing to him, being changed by him into his likeness, and waiting patiently for their turn to come to go to heaven. That number too is growing by the thousands every single day as new people give their lives to Christ and the church grows numerically right across the world. Strong and permanent, this Jesus is well able to keep his own.

There are some remarkable bronze statues which have lasted for thousands of years. The equestrian statue of Marcus Aurelius which is larger than life size is in remarkably good condition despite having been cast in 175 AD, now on display in the Capitoline Museums in Rome. Similarly, the four bronze horses made in the second century AD and brought from Constantinople to decorate St Mark's Church in Venice. Bronze work has longevity built into it because of its resistance to corrosion.

Jesus' bronze feet speak of permanence. For all the challenging, attacking, opposing, undermining, denying, and questioning, Jesus, and his teachings remain in perfect condition two thousand years after they were given. How we need to hear this when certain emphases of Biblical Christianity are being ferociously opposed. There is pressure from outside the church and sometimes cowardice and betrayal from within the church. The pressure is on us to compromise, but Jesus has bronze feet and we need to develop that resistance to corrosion which is part of his own character.

As a young Christian I remember hearing that if we cut out a block of truth then our opponents will simply blunt their arrows on it, for truth remains true even if no-one believes it. A.W.Tozer in his book *The Knowledge of the Holy* (1961) has a chapter on the immutability of God. That may be a new word to some of us and one that we don't particularly want to learn, but it simply means unchanging. God is unchanging. The Bible repeatedly insists that God does not change. He is not fickle or unreliable. He doesn't say one thing today and another thing tomorrow. He doesn't change his mind on the things that he has already said. He is not the victim of fashions or bandwagons.

Change may be the bread and butter of the clothing industry, it may be the latest promotion of a political party but God says of himself, 'I the Lord do not change'.[3] If we were to walk away from God for a thousand years and come back to him again a thousand years later then we would find that he was the very same God to whom we returned as the one that we had left. Balaam, the scurrilous prophet of ancient times was given a message for the pagan king who had hired him, and the message was this, 'God is not human, that he should lie, not a human being, that he should change his mind.'[4] We Christians are so often accused of creating a God in our own image, but the Lord rejects such an idea completely. The contrasts between us and him could not be starker. We change like the wind, but he is steady, consistent and 'immutable'.

Change in human beings is impossible to escape as we grow and age. Our appetites change, our attitudes change, our outlooks change, our aspirations change, our bodies change, but change in God is impossible to conceive. How could he change? Because all change is qualitative, it is either from better to worse or from worse to better, it is either from immaturity to maturity or from maturity to immaturity. If God changes, then in which direction is he going? Would it have been better to have lived with him in the past, or will he be a better God in the years that lie ahead, more benign and accepting at some time in the future? When would it be

---

[3] Malachi 3:6.
[4] Numbers 23:19.

best to belong to him? But James, the brother of Jesus squashes such an idea when he writes, 'Every good and perfect gift is from above, coming down from the Father of the heavenly lights, who does not change like shifting shadows.'[5]

God doesn't change in his being nor does he change in his moods. We are so familiar with having to tiptoe around one another at certain times of the day. The friend who isn't fully awake until the second coffee at 10 am.; the recluse who has a constant need for solitude to get some extra head space; the volatile person who is different today from yesterday. Not Jesus, there is no corrosion associated with his bronze feet. He is the same always. Boring, will be the cry of the youngster. Not at all. This is precisely the God that we need. Constant, reliable, rock-steady, and true.

This extends to his moral standards too. Not so long ago I attended a registry office wedding and at the beginning the registrar read out some information about the law regarding marriage as it applies in Britain today. But it was clear from what she was reading that the current law is entirely dependent upon the government of the day and that if the government changed, or attitudes changed, then the laws on marriage might change too. Nothing is fixed. Yet because God doesn't change his mind, because he's not a fickle human being, his standards are the same for all people in all cultures for all time. His moral laws may have been codified four thousand years ago during the time of Moses but they are relevant to our society four thousand years later and will continue to be relevant and applicable in four thousand years from now. Society will not have evolved to such an extent that we will need new and different standards to live by.

Wonderfully, God's attitudes don't change either. He continues to be constant in his faithfulness to his people, his compassion to the needy, his concern for the lost, his love for all. He's constant in his

---

[5] James 1:17.

hostility to sin which has been the same from the very beginning. He's constant in his solution to human sin which is available through the cross of Jesus, and only through his cross. It's on offer to us as ever once more today. He's the Jesus with the bronze feet which now have nail marks in them although those were not mentioned by John on this occasion.

I keep coming across Christians who are increasingly insecure about the things that they believe. Many are feeling that the sustained attack from a culture which is becoming more and more hostile and aggressive towards Christianity is draining them. They are fatigued in their discipleship, wondering how long they can hold on and becoming increasingly intimidated and silenced. They dare not say anything about their faith in public because of the storm and cancellation which would follow any strong clear Christian statement. But Jesus has got bronze feet. There is no metal fatigue here and there's no need for fatigue in our Christian discipleship because again and again the message of Jesus has conquered.

A few years ago there was an article in the *Cambrian News* in Aberystwyth about a group of pagans who were meeting in the town. I was phoned for comment because this was just the kind of unusual thing that the media love to highlight. My response was that there was no need for concern. Paganism had been in the ascendant in Wales one thousand seven hundred years ago. It met Christianity face to face and had to retreat until the whole of Wales was Christian.

There was a time when the Greek religion dominated the ancient Mediterranean world. It was so admired that the Roman empire imitated, adapted and adopted its mythology. But eventually it was completely eradicated by the Christian message and what remains is of interest only to academic historians in universities who like to study ancient thought. Today, nobody believes the religious teachings that the ancient Greeks so energetically promoted around their world.

There is a prophetic promise written down by Paul the apostle that the day is coming when 'at the name of Jesus, every knee will bow, in heaven and on earth and under the earth.'[6] There is no religion which does not give way to Jesus, and today right across the world on every continent members of other religions are turning to him and becoming his disciples. Buddhism, Hinduism, Islam, are all yielding new followers to Jesus Christ, so we should not allow ourselves to be silenced or fatigued in the battle for the Christian faith. The day will come when the 'woke' secular fashion will be a thing of the past, we should remember that Jesus is equal to every competition. We belong to the Jesus of the bronze feet, not the feet of clay.

One other feature of Jesus' feet which John noticed was that they looked as though they were 'glowing in a furnace.'[7] That suggests not only that they were freshly made, but more particularly that they were free from impurity, perfect and flawless; they couldn't be improved upon. King David writing in one of his psalms declares, 'The words of the LORD are flawless, like silver purified in a crucible, like gold refined seven times.'[8] How could anything that has been refined seven times in a furnace possibly have any impurity remaining in it?

David goes on to say, 'As for God, his way is perfect: The LORD's word is flawless; he shields all who take refuge in him.'[9] Here is David's logic, because the Lord is perfect in all he does, then he's also perfect in everything that he says. Isn't that absolutely true of Jesus when we look at him again? His character was tested by fire.

---

[6] Philippians 2:10.
[7] Revelation 1:15.
[8] Psalm 12:6.
[9] Psalm 18:30.

At the very worst moment in his earthly life as they hammered nails through his flesh, instead of screaming for revenge he prayed for forgiveness for the soldiers, 'Father forgive them, for they do not know what they are doing'.[10]

Jesus had a ministry which was tested by fire. He didn't fail in that ministry on one single occasion. He healed the sick, he cast out demons, he raised the dead. There was no one who was brought to him whom he did not help.[11] He gave teaching which was tested by fire in the face of debate, and discussion, in the face of contempt and ridicule, in the face of scepticism and downright opposition. But then he made this startling claim when on trial for his life before Pontius Pilate, 'Everyone on the side of truth listens to me.'[12]

When we look again at Jesus, at his life, his character, his ministry, his teaching, and its content, it is flawless. It and he still stand supreme. He, his truth, his kingdom will endure for eternity. We can be assured and confident in our faith. We can believe with authority and speak with authority, and if we need re-assurance then just look at his feet.

Thinking moment

- Is it right that an unchanging God is the kind of God that we need? What would be the outcome of a God who changed over the millennia?

- Have we found ourselves silenced and intimidated by the changes in attitudes in the society around us? Is there anything we can do to become more courageous than we have been?

---

[10] Luke 23:34.
[11] Matthew 4:24.
[12] John 18:37.

- The Lord's word is flawless. That is a statement which would be energetically contested today. How might we defend such a statement?

Chapter 6

A must-listen voice (Revelation 1:15b)

'His voice was like the sound of rushing waters. In his right hand he held seven stars' (Revelation 1:15f)

Mercifully it rarely happens these days but there was a time when people would ring each other and instead of giving their name they would ask, 'Do you know who's speaking?' You'd then have to play a guessing game until either you got it right or they identified themselves. Interestingly, when Jesus speaks to John in his vision he doesn't give his name. He identifies himself by the sound of his voice, by its tone and by the content of what he has to say. But in fact Jesus was not inviting John into a conversation with him, he was giving him a series of revelations as well as a number of commands.

There is absolutely no limit whatsoever to the way in which the Lord can get our attention. The Bible gives illustration after illustration of him speaking to human beings in the most extraordinary of circumstances. In the book of Exodus we read of him speaking out of a bush which is on fire but which doesn't burn up in the Sinai desert.[1] Moses is the one who is being spoken to. Perhaps the most amusing is the experience of Balaam, a scurrilous prophet, who after being stopped in his tracks by an angel is then spoken to through a donkey.[2] One of the most poignant is Elijah back on the mountain where the Lord had met Moses and where he hears a voice speaking to him in a gentle whisper.[3] That's closest to my own experience for when the Lord brought me to himself he did it through his whisper in my conscience. There was no brilliant

---

[1] Exodus 3:4.
[2] Numbers 22.
[3] 1 Kings 19:12.

and persuasive sermon, no insightful counsellor, no earnest evangelist. It was just between the Lord and me, and after I had given in and become a disciple people were asking me, 'What's happened to you?' It had all happened in secret.

Every one of us has a different story to tell of the way that the Lord broke into our lives and brought us to himself. That's what makes it so interesting to listen to other Christians telling their stories. Not one of them is the same as another. As we all have different fingerprints on our hands, so we all have different fingerprints of God upon our souls.

One of my friends was looking forward to his eightieth birthday with enormous anticipation, not because he was expecting great celebrations with his family but because he is still an ardent competitor in athletics. He has cupboards and drawers full of medals and cups and trophies, many of them inscribed with the date and place of the competition. On his eightieth birthday, he moved into a new category of competitors from being the oldest in the seventy-five to seventy-nine age group to being the youngest in the eighty to eighty-five grouping, and that of course would increase his chances of more trophies to add to his collection. We are trophies of the Lord and inscribed upon us are the dates and place when he won us to himself.

When we are praying for family members and friends over a period of decades, maybe even a lifetime, there's no need for us to give the Lord instructions about how he is to draw someone to himself. He has a multiplicity of methods available and he'll choose which ever one is appropriate to the person and the occasion. Just yesterday as I'm writing this, a friend sent a Whatsapp message to say that someone for whom he'd been praying for twenty-six years had called by to say that he had come to faith. That's what we want to hear. How it happens and who is involved, if anyone, is irrelevant to the outcome although it's always fascinating to hear the details.

When the Lord speaks to John at the beginning of his vision it is with a voice which is like a trumpet blast.[4] This is a 'Hey!' moment. The Lord wants John's attention and he gets it. When John turns around the Lord has achieved his first objective, John's full and undivided attention. But then he moderates his voice. He doesn't need to speak to him with the sound of a trumpet any more. His voice changes and it's now like the 'sound of rushing waters'.[5] This is a divine voice and John knows it because as we've already noted he was a man who knew his Bible. Ezekiel, the prophet in ancient times had seen the glory of God coming into the temple of Jerusalem and as he comes there's a corresponding sound of his voice as he speaks over the temple and the city. This is how Ezekiel describes what he saw and heard, 'I saw the glory of the God of Israel coming from the east. His voice was like the roar of rushing waters.'[6] John was hearing again in his own time the ancient voice of God, ever contemporary, ever new, in just the same way as previously Ezekiel had heard him all those years before.

Some have thought that the noise of this voice might have resembled the crashing sound of waves on the coastline of the small island of Patmos which must have dominated the lives of those who lived there. But more likely it is the sound of a torrent, a cascade, a flood of water which is dominant above all other sounds and cuts off conversation of any kind. Nothing else can be heard above the sound of the waters. How appropriate because the Lord's voice carries with it authority. It is a commanding voice. It's not to be debated, but to be obeyed. It's a voice which has the final word. And our human pride is resistant to such a concept. We are the ones who want to have the final word, but we can't when the final word is spoken by a divine voice. That voice trumps all others, ours included.

---

[4] Revelation 1:10.
[5] Revelation 1:15.
[6] Ezekiel 43:2.

There is one simple reason why the city of Jerusalem grew up in the barren mountains of Judea: the Gihon Spring. For centuries, there has been sufficient water flowing naturally from the spring to supply the needs of two and a half thousand people without needing any additional water source. Prior to people coming to live close to the place where the spring emerged fully formed from under the earth, the water from the spring would have flowed down to the Jordan valley. Wherever it flowed there would have been a ribbon of green as the water would have sustained life, grassland, pasture, cultivation. Wherever water goes something happens.

Jesus' voice is a happening voice. We know that it is creative for God himself created all that exists by his commanding word. That creativity continues to be manifested whenever the voice of Jesus is heard. Never before this vision had Jesus declared his specific, individual and personal interest in the progress of seven of his churches, giving an indication of his heart towards every church around the world in every age. Never before this vision had Jesus given such a clear insight to his people into what is going on in heaven in the detail which is recorded in the subsequent revelations given to John. Never before had Jesus given such detailed insights into the way in which the history of this world is going to unfold. This is all new, unprecedented, and enormously valuable to us, his disciples in succeeding generations. It's what makes the book of Revelation into such a superb concluding book of the Bible.

But more immediately the happening voice commands John to write down what he sees. This is not just for his personal consumption and encouragement. This is for all Christians for all time until the end finally comes. So, John, write what you see.[7] If he doesn't understand what's required of him the first time that he receives the command, then he's told a second time. He's got something to do as a result of the revelation. So have we. The intention of it is motivational. It has been given to strengthen us,

---

[7] Revelation 1:11 and 19.

to give us focus and hope, to stiffen our resolve in the face of opposition. Life is difficult but it is nonetheless under the Lordship of Christ. Life feels unpredictable but in fact the future is very predictable indeed. God wins! We fear for the future. Don't! Time is moving forward under heaven's control.

Here's the thread which needs to be emphasised again and again. 'Do not be afraid.'[8] Do not be afraid of the Jesus you are seeing in the vision, for he is for you. Do not be afraid of the circumstances which surround you because you are not alone, Jesus is the Living One. Do not be afraid about the outcome of world events, because the end of the story has already been written and it has a good outcome. Evil dies. Good triumphs.

Thinking moment

- Have you had some 'Hey!' moments in your life? Have you ever shared them with others for their encouragement?

- 'A voice which is not to be debated but obeyed.' Why do we have such difficulty in submitting ourselves to the voice of the Lord, or is it just me?

- Does this vision of Jesus address your fears at all? How can you get these truths so embedded in your soul that your anxieties begin to become less?

---

[8] Revelation 1:17.

Chapter 7

A star-gazing Jesus (Revelation 1:16a)

'In his right hand he held seven stars, and coming out of his mouth was a sharp, double-edged sword' (Revelation 1:16)

When my wife and I go on a long journey to somewhere we've not been before, or are about to start on a complicated trip of some kind, we often ask the Lord to send angels to help us. We're not expecting the heavenly kind with wings, but rather some kind-hearted person who'll take time to point us in the right direction and help us when we get lost or confused. It's been quite remarkable over the years how often those prayers have been answered, even to the extent of saying occasionally to someone, 'You are our angel for the day'. Some people seem pleased at such a comment whilst others are rather nonplussed.

John describes Jesus as having seven stars in his right hand[1] and the meaning of the stars would have remained a mystery to us and a subject of speculation had Jesus not explained what they were. He tells us that the seven stars are 'the angels (*aggelos*) of the seven churches.'[2]

There's a great deal of interest in angels amongst 'New Age' people, so we must be careful that we stay close to what we are told about the angels and their role in the Scriptures. If Jesus is referring to the heavenly angels here, then there are some quite precious truths for us to hold on to.

As the revelation unfolds, John is commanded to write to seven different angels who each appear to have a role in one of the

---

[1] Revelation 1:16.
[2] Revelation 1:20.

churches in Asia Minor which are recipients of John's letters. Never before, or since (so far as we know) has a human being been involved in the 'administrative' work of heaven. If God wanted to speak to an angel and give that angel a specific instruction then he most certainly doesn't need a human intermediary. Yet here God addresses John, a human being, who is then to address an angel, a heavenly being on behalf of God. It's the first and only time that we read of this in the Bible, but that doesn't make it untrue. It only makes it unique. There are plenty of other unique events described in the Bible.

But this event, if it is a correct interpretation, does two things. Firstly, it emphasises the dignity of human beings, for we have been made 'a little lower than the angels.'[3] We easily forget our place in the scheme of things and need to be reminded of where we fit in God's creation. We are not just sophisticated primates at a level a little above the animal kingdom. We are creatures of great worth and status, which is made all the more extraordinary when we are invited into the service of Almighty God. How could we humans ever be given a greater honour?

Secondly, because John is to pass on Jesus' own interest in and concern for these seven churches the content of what he writes is on display for all to see. It becomes something which is available for public consumption, not just privately for each individual church, even though some of them might have preferred for no one else to hear what Jesus had to say to them. As a result, these seven letters have been a source of inspiration and guidance for the whole church for centuries.[4]

What then is the role of these angels in the churches of Asia Minor? The fact that Jesus is sending them an 'open letter'

---

[3] Psalm 8:5.

[4] See John Stott. *What Christ Thinks of the Church: Preaching from Revelation 1 to 3.*British Commonwealth ed. (Milton Keynes, ©1990)

dictated to John and written down for them to read suggests that they have some responsibility for protection, guidance and support of each individual congregation. There is even a sense of accountability on the part of the angel on the one hand to each of the churches and on the other hand to the Lord himself. This is the Lord speaking to John who is speaking to both the angel of the church and to the congregation itself. If children have guardian angels and Jesus spoke about them suggesting that each child has a corresponding angel in heaven appointed to them to care for their well-being[5] then it should come as no surprise that a congregation of Christians should be similarly cared for and cared about.

There's an amusing event in the Acts of the Apostles when Peter has been released from prison in Jerusalem in the middle of the night by the intervention of an angel. His chains have fallen from his wrists and the prison gates have opened without a key being turned in the lock. The angel leaves him and Peter finds himself alone on the streets of Jerusalem and heads straight for the house of Mary, the mother of John Mark. When he knocks on the outer gate of the house and calls out to be let in, the servant girl Rhoda rushes inside to tell the members of an all-night prayer meeting that Peter is at the gate. Their response is interesting because they don't believe it could be him and they say, 'It must be his angel.'[6]

An angel for children, an angel for an apostle, so why not an angel for each congregation? That puts a new perspective perhaps on our own local church and the provision that the Lord has made for us, for our protection and for our welfare. There is no suggestion that we should attempt to identify these angels or contact them or pray to them, but simply that we should take pleasure in their existence as part of the enveloping love of Jesus for his people. After all, he said that he could command twelve legions of angels for his own personal defence on the day of his trial.[7] That's sixty thousand in

---

[5] Matthew 18:10.
[6] Acts 12:15.

all. They must surely be invincible with all of the resources of heaven behind them, but then so too are we. What resources we have available to us including angelic ones which we cannot see and which all too frequently we never take into account.

What's particularly impressive about John's vision is that Jesus is holding these seven angelic stars in his right hand.[8] The churches are scattered over a wide geographical area but the angels are kept on the palm of his hand. They are entirely at his disposal and under his authority. They are immediately available to him to do his bidding but simultaneously they are protected by him as they might be detailed to protect others. The stars give light too, but as their light is eclipsed every day by the light of the sun, so too the light of the angels is rightly eclipsed by the light of the Son. He is the one who draws our attention and he is the one who outshines all others.

Another translation of the word *aggelos* in other parts of the Bible is the title messenger. Some Bible students have suggested that John was not commanded to write to heavenly angels but that he was hosting a meeting of senior church leaders or bishops from the seven different congregations on the island of Patmos during his exile and that he was passing on to them what he believed the Lord was saying to him. If that is correct, then there are still some stimulating truths here for us. A picture of seven senior church leaders being held in the palm of the right hand of Jesus. It speaks of his favour towards them, their preciousness in his eyes, and their absolute security as it would be impossible for anyone to snatch them out of his hand. That was a firm promise of Jesus to his people.[9]

---

[7] Matthew 26:53.
[8] Revelation 1:16.
[9] John 10:28.)

Either way, angels or bishops, the Lord is gloriously in control. The stars were his creation and he called them into being. The Lord draws Job's attention to the wonders of the night sky when he's depressed and questioning the purpose of his existence.

> Can you bind the beautiful Pleiades? Can you loose the cords of Orion? Can you bring forth the constellations in their seasons or lead out the Bear with its cubs? Do you know the laws of the heavens? Can you set up God's dominion over the earth?[10]

The answer to all of those questions is a straight 'No!' All of these things are outside of the power of Job to initiate them or to control them, but all of these things are well within the control of Almighty God. So too, the creation of angels and the directing of them in their heavenly duties. So too, the calling of church leaders and the directing of them in their earthly duties.

Thinking moment

- How can we get a good balance in our thinking about angels neither ignoring their existence on the one hand, nor becoming preoccupied with them on the other?

- If the church leadership is held securely in the Lord's hand so that no one can snatch them away, then how is it that we have been let down by so many leaders in recent times? Is his holding power limited in some way?

- How much does the invincibility of the powers of heaven spill over into our lives? Should it? Should we expect more of that victory in our own daily experience?

---

[10] Job 38:31-33. *The Thompson Chain Reference Bible*: New International Version. (Indianapolis, Ind: B B Kirkbride Bible Co, ©1990

Chapter 8

A sharp-tongued Jesus (Revelation 1:16b)

'Coming out of his mouth was a sharp, double-edged sword. His face was like the sun shining in all its brilliance.' (Revelation 1:16)

One of things that Covid taught us very clearly is that we lip-read much more than we think. With masks on, everyone needed to turn up the volume of their voice by several decibels. Firstly, because the mask had the effect of smothering the voice but secondly, because we couldn't see the speaker's lips. 'Read my lips' is more than a cheeky way of telling someone to trust you, much of the time it is a necessity in the process of communication with one another.

In his vision John hears the voice of the Lord from behind him. To begin with it startles him because it's like the sound of a trumpet but subsequently it impresses him because it continues like the sound of rushing water. But as with all of us as John listens to what Jesus has to say he begins to read his lips and what he sees next is disturbing. Instead of a tongue, he sees a 'sharp doubled-edged sword' protruding from Jesus' mouth.

We know well enough that different swords are chosen depending on the battle that is to be fought. A cavalry soldier will use a sabre when he is on horseback. It has just one sharp edge and is used for slashing downwards. In a battle on foot a soldier might use a broadsword with the intention of standing at a distance to fight. The Roman soldiers were equipped with a short double-edged sword which was tongue-like and used for close combat. Jesus with a Roman-style sword for a tongue is not a cuddly picture. Swords were and are weapons of offence.

In years of parish visiting, I've come across people with razor-sharp tongues. You need body armour in order to visit them and you never know which direction the attack is going to come from or how quickly the knife will be unsheathed. It always seems to be at the ready. As I recall, it didn't take much effort to find an excuse to postpone a visit to such people until another day. They were best avoided. But is that what Jesus is like? Combative, cutting, argumentative, aggressive, offensive and best avoided? That's what the image of a sharp sword for a tongue suggests.

It is true that there is a side of Jesus which is dangerous and many people have realised that, which is why they try to keep him at arm's length. But the sword of Jesus' tongue is wielded skilfully, with the intention of giving life, not of taking it away; with the intention of producing beneficial results; to heal, not to wound; to build up, not to destroy. The letter to the Hebrews picks up this theme when it says, 'The Word of God is alive and active and sharper than any double-edged sword; it penetrates even to dividing soul and spirit; joint and marrow, it judges the thoughts and attitudes of the heart.'[1]

Sword drill for a Roman soldier would take hours every day. There would be nothing clumsy about the way that the soldiers handled their swords. They would operate with surgical precision. The thrust, the parry, the strike, the slash would all be practised and practised, so that when in battle the sword's use was the work of a specialist. Is it conceivable that the sword of God's Word would be wielded less skilfully by Jesus than the sword of a Roman soldier?

The Word of God is going to divide soul and spirit, says the letter to the Hebrews. But there is no specialist or surgeon who is so skilled in anatomy and dissection that they can tell us where to insert the knife and where the soul begins and the spirit ends. Such

---

[1] Hebrews 4:12.

an operation surely requires the greatest possible precision and yet there is only one person who knows how to perform it. How was it done? Many of us as we think this over can say that though we do not understand it, yet we have experienced what the Bible describes which are the words of Jesus penetrating to the very deepest parts of our being and digging deep within us into the conscience, into the heart, into the soul with surgical skill.

There was a time when the things of God were a complete irrelevance in our lives, when Jesus and his teachings were of no more importance than the writings of Spike Milligan But since then, the skilled swordsman has gone to work on our lives and penetrated our souls and brought us light, understanding, reality, truth, experience and so much more.

We're also told that the Word of God can divide joints and marrow. Now that is something much easier for a surgeon. These are parts of the human anatomy that can be identified and dealt with. But what we are hearing here is that the Bible could potentially have physical effects upon us. And again, that is absolutely true. Some of us have experienced that effect. 'Those who wait upon the Lord will renew their strength',[2] says Isaiah. We have waited and we have been strengthened. The promise corresponds to our experience. 'Come to me all those who are weary and heavy-laden and I will give you rest',[3] said Jesus. We have come and we have been given rest. Emotional, psychological, spiritual, physical rest. Soul rest, just as he said. 'Comfort, comfort my people, says your God'.[4] And they have been comforted and they are comforted now. The truths of Scripture when they are believed, inhabited, received, trusted, can and do have physical effects.

---

[2] Isaiah 40:31.
[3] Matthew 11:28.
[4] Isaiah 40:1.

But there is more because the Word of God judges the thoughts and attitudes of the heart. The very part of us that no one else knows is like an open book to the Lord. That part of us which is kept concealed beneath layers upon layers of convention, culture, acceptable behaviour and outward conformity, beneath further layers of secrecy and concealment: the Lord is able to address our secret world, to expose it, to lay it bare, to unmask it, to declare it as fully known when he deals with us. He has done that to so many, as he has awakened the conscience. But there is no mechanism known to man that can do this. There are no X-rays, no scans, or ultrasounds which can penetrate the thoughts and attitudes of a person's inner life, but the Lord can do it, and does do it; sometimes without our permission or co-operation. Many of us have had the experience of a passage in the Bible suddenly coming alive, or a comment in a sermon, or a part of a conversation which has gripped us and quite unexpectedly our concealment has been stripped away and the Lord has thrust right into the heart of our problems like a rapier thrust.

That was precisely what happened as a result of Peter's sermon on the Day of Pentecost. He had been speaking to a large crowd about the crucifixion of Jesus. The Jewish authorities had convicted Jesus during their charade of a trial and Pontius Pilate had condemned him to death and executed him, but the residents of Jerusalem were complicit because they hadn't stopped it from happening and Peter presses that fact home in his address. 'You, with the help of wicked men put him to death by nailing him to the cross.'[5] Peter goes for the jugular without embarrassment, and the result was the deepest possible conviction of heart. 'When the people heard this they were cut to the heart and said, 'Brothers, what shall we do?''[6]

---

[5] Acts 2:23.
[6] Acts 2:37.

Do we presume that Jesus is less skilled with his scalpel than any surgeon? The image of Jesus wielding a sword for the purpose of giving life is counter-intuitive. Swords are for maiming, for wounding, for killing and the problems with this image are not easily dispelled for it's still intimidating, threatening, unsettling. Yet, perhaps to some degree it needs to be both disturbing and challenging. We know well enough that we are much more likely to cut ourselves shaving with a blunt razor than with a sharp one. The greater danger is with the blunt razor because it won't cut our whiskers, but it may well cut our skin if we're not careful as we try to shave away our stubble.

Every time we see Jesus in action in the New Testament it is with razor-sharp insight, razor-sharp commentary and a razor-sharp response to the needs of the people that he meets. There is the well-known example of an interview with a man who comes to talk to Jesus about eternal life.[7] The man has five things that Jesus surely would want in any disciple. He has youth on his side, he's from a good family, he's clearly an influencer of others, he has money and he's spiritually hungry. What else would he need to become an impressive new recruit? But here comes the sword. Your money is getting in the way of your soul. 'Sell everything you have, give to the poor. Then come and follow me.'[8]

What have we heard? 'The Word of God judges the thoughts and attitudes of the heart'. Jesus was right, wasn't he? Yes, he was right in his assessment of where this young man stood spiritually, but surely that's not the way to handle people? After all he didn't become a disciple. He went away disappointed and who can be surprised? Doesn't Jesus need to learn to be a bit more subtle in the way that he deals with people? No, Jesus loves us enough to tell us the truth. The world needs more of it not less. 'Wounds from a friend can be trusted but an enemy multiplies kisses.'[9]

---

[7] Luke 18:18ff.
[8] Matthew 19:21.

Jesus was involved in a theological debate about the afterlife and what happens once we have passed into the next life. He is debating with the Sadducees who took a liberal line on the interpretation of the Scriptures. Theirs was a non-miraculous, non-spiritual religion. It was all down to how you lived your life. As the discussion proceeds Jesus said to them 'You are in error because you don't know the Scriptures or the power of God.'[10] That's hardly winsome. In fact it's on the borderline of being offensive. Doesn't Jesus realise that he's not just got to win the argument but he's got to win his opponent too, and probably in reverse order, Yet in debate, discussion, preaching and personal interviews Jesus holds to a single important principle and that is to 'speak the truth in love.'[11] He does it with everyone, including us. Thank God for that.

Some years ago, I had been invited to contribute a chapter to a book of essays on church life. I put the last full stop at the end of my contribution and took it around to three friends for their comments. Two of them said how good it was but the third had something else to say. I can still recall the embarrassment and uncertainty in his eyes as he told me that what I had written was dull and lifeless and that I could do much better than that. What a good friend he was. Similarly, in the early days of learning the Welsh language there were those around me who wanted to encourage me every time I ventured to use my Welsh in conversation. They were full of praise and affirmation. But the best tutors were those who told me that I was speaking translated English and that I needed to learn to speak more colloquially. Those are the kind of people we need around us. That's the kind of Jesus we need, and gloriously that's the kind of Jesus we have. He has a tongue the shape of a double-edged sword.

---

[9] Proverbs 27:6.
[10] Matthew 22:29.
[11] Ephesians 4:15.

He will not spare our feelings. He will not beat about the bush. He invites us to repent when we come to him rather than drift rather aimlessly into his kingdom on a cloud of emotion. He does not have a bland Gospel for us but one with razor sharp edges. He is not a master of ambiguity. That's the world of comedians with their *double entendre.* That's the world of politicians and diplomats trying to get a negotiated settlement. That's the world, tragically, of some religious leaders trying to persuade people who fundamentally disagree to walk together but it is not the world of Jesus.

Jesus was direct, straightforward and simple in his teaching so that he could be understood by all. It has long been said that if he didn't mean what he said, then why on earth didn't he say what he meant? The issue with Jesus is not interpreting what he said, but obeying what he said. There's a lovely conversation recorded of two boys and their father:

'Dad, please can we go out to play in the garden?'
'No, boys you can't. Supper will be ready in twenty minutes, so there isn't time.'
'Oh Dad, please', say the boys.
'No, boys you can't. Mum has worked hard to get a good meal for us and we must be at the table on time.'
'Oh Dad. Just for a little while.'
'No, in ten minutes I'm going to ask you to lay the table.'
'Oh Dad.'
'No, if you go out now I'll be calling you in straight away to change your shoes and wash your hands. You can't go outside now.'
As the boys leave the room one says to the other, 'That was a yes, wasn't it?'

When the Bible says no, time after time it's not a matter of interpretation but of obedience. Leonard Ravenhill, church leader and preacher who died in the 1990s wrote 'One of these days some simple soul will pick up the book of God and read it, and believe it. The rest of us will be embarrassed. We have adopted the convenient theory that the Bible is a book to be explained, whereas first and foremost it is a book to be believed, and after that to be obeyed.'[12]

If we expect a Jesus who is cuddly, bland and inoffensive then it would be better if we did not read the New Testament at all, for that is not the Jesus we find there. If we want a Jesus who always says yes to us then we'd better pray to someone else because the Jesus whom John saw in his vision was not like that then and he isn't like that now for one reason and one reason only. He wants our best.

In another illustration that Jesus used, he spoke about a sharp cutting tool being in the hands of God the Father. The picture is of a vine which is trailing its way over the house. It's that time of the year when the vine needs some attention before it gets out of hand and becomes unproductive. Jesus describes himself as the vine and says that it is God the Father who is going to cut away at the vine in order to ensure that it is as fruitful as it can possibly be. The vine has not been grown as a hobby nor for decoration. The gardener is single-minded about the vine. He wants it to produce grapes for him, grapes of quality and in substantial quantities.

Vines are vigorous plants but they are also unruly. If they aren't pruned severely, then a potentially abundant harvest will be lost. In his illustration Jesus makes it plain that every disciple needs pruning in order to maximise the potential which is locked away inside each of us. Without it, Jesus suggests that there would be no

---

[12] Quoted by Dick Eastman *The Hour that Changes the World: a practical plan for personal prayer.* (Grand Rapids, Mich. Baker Book House, ©1978.) p.54.

progress in godliness or holiness, obedience, servanthood or compassion.

When the gardener sees that there are fruit-producing buds on the branch, he'll cut away everything beyond those buds to ensure that all the nourishment of the branch goes into the fruit and is not drained away into wasted leaves or more branches. What is the divine gardener looking for in our lives? The fruit of godly character and Christian love. He's happy to cut away everything that distracts from that. He's happy to put all of his energies into producing more in us. He'll wield the sword, the knife, the razor on us, in us and through us in order to make that into something which happens.

Thinking moment

- A sharp-tongued Jesus. Isn't that a contradiction in terms?

- Are you able to detect evidence of the gardener at work in and on your life?

- Have you had experiences in your life when you were 'pruned' by what happened to you? Have you been able to look back at those experiences with thankfulness?

Chapter 9

A sunshine-faced Jesus (Revelation 1:16c)

'His face was like the sun shining in all its brilliance. When I saw him, I fell at his feet as though dead' (Revelation 1:16f)

Apparently, it only takes seven seconds to make a first impression on another human being. When we meet people for the first time, we make quick decisions about them based on their eye contact, their appearance, their handshake, and other verbal and non-verbal cues. John has this vision of Jesus and it must have persisted for some time for him to take in so many of his attributes. What is surprising is that the sunshine face of Jesus is the last in his list, particularly as it was brilliant in its impact.

Perhaps the reason that he leaves it until last is the fact that this is not the first time that he has seen Jesus with a brilliantly shining face. That's precisely what he had seen before on Mount Hermon at Jesus' transfiguration. He, together with Peter and James his own brother, had accompanied Jesus on a climb up the mountain. Whilst they were there another one of those unrepeated events took place. Unexpectedly and without warning or preparation, Jesus was 'transfigured' as they looked on. There was a transformation in him which they found hard to describe and put into words. 'His face shone like the sun, and his robes became as white as the light.'[1] Jesus went from being ordinarily human to being gloriously human. It was as though a curtain had been pulled back to allow these three disciples to see something that they couldn't see before. A face shining like the sun is part of the revelation.

But that is far from the end of what they see, for the number of people on the mountain suddenly increased from four to six. Jesus

---

[1] Matthew 17:2.

plus three disciples, but now also joined by Moses and Elijah. It doesn't seem as though they need any introduction. They appear to be immediately recognisable. Moses represents the law which had been given through him to the Children of Israel and Elijah represents the many prophets who had given inspired guidance to the nation over the centuries. There was a sense of completeness therefore with Jesus and Moses and Elijah holding a conversation together. Everything that had been written about him as the Messiah who was to come is now being fulfilled in Jesus.

Yet still the climax of the event has not yet come. 'A bright cloud enveloped them, and a voice from the cloud said, 'This is my Son whom I love; with him I am well pleased. Listen to him!' If there was ever a moment of reassurance, of undeniable evidence, this was the moment for these three disciples to know for sure that Jesus was (and is) the Son of the Living God. That had been the conclusion of the evidence that they had already seen and it was Peter's declaration which he had made very shortly before this experience, but now they have conclusive evidence to give them greater confidence still. They have a voice from heaven, the appearance of Moses and Elijah, they have Jesus in shining clothes and they see him with a face that shines like the sun in all its brilliance. So when John sees Jesus again in his vision shining in precisely the same way, he can say to himself, 'Seen it before!' This is not new for him, but it is yet one more confirmation, if he needed it, that the one in front of him now in this vision on the island of Patmos was the very same Jesus whom he knew sixty years before.

There is no attempt by John to describe the physical features of Jesus face, only the fact that his face shone like the sun. In fact, all of the physical descriptions that we have read and seen in paintings are entirely fanciful and contrived. There is no surviving eye-witness account of Jesus' appearance, yet here the over-riding impression that John conveys is of his brilliant holiness. We are warned not to look directly at the sun because of the damage this could do to our eyes, and we know from experience that it's almost impossible to do it anyway. To try to look directly at Jesus is to look into his brilliant holiness which both attracts us and humbles us at the same time.

The fascinating thing about the worship of heaven is that it is completely absorbed with the holiness of God. Both in the Old Testament and in the New whenever anyone is given an opportunity to glimpse into heaven and see what is going on there, all of the residents of heaven are doing exactly the same thing. They are celebrating the holiness of God. That is what Isaiah saw when he was given a vision of heaven. The angels were worshipping and celebrating the holiness of God. 'Holy, holy, holy is the Lord Almighty; the whole earth is full of his glory.'[2] They are not singing of his love or his mercy or his grace or his compassion or his glory, or anything else but only of his holiness. That's precisely what John sees later on in his own revelation as his vision progresses. Hundreds of years have passed between Isaiah and John yet we are told that 'Day and night the angels never stop saying: 'Holy, holy, holy is the Lord God Almighty.'[3]

There is something of immense importance here. For the holiness of God is his chief characteristic. It is the holiness of God which holds the whole of his character in balance. It is the keystone in the arch of God's own being. His love for us is holy love, so it is neither over-indulgent on the one hand nor overly severe on the other. His justice is holy so that it is perfectly balanced, fully understanding extenuating circumstances whilst also seeing through our attempts at excuses. His mercy towards us is holy, so it does not sweep our sins under the carpet or turn a blind eye to what we have done wrong, rather it deals with our sins at the cross with full atonement paid for each one of them. If God were not holy, then he would not be a God worth worshipping. It God were

[2] Isaiah 6:3.
[3] Revelation 4:8.

not holy, then the universe would collapse for it entirely depends upon his consistency of character.

As is the Father, so too is the Son. 'This is my Son, whom I love.' All of the characteristics of the Father are to be seen in the Son, so when he appears in his glory on the Mount of Transfiguration he has a face which shines like the sun, and when he appears in his glory in John's vision on Patmos, he has a face which shines like the sun again. His perfection makes him so attractive. There is a longing which has been placed within us, something of that original image of God in which we were created and which still persists. It is a longing for that same perfection and holiness. We admire it in him and we desire to be like him. We haven't worked that up inside ourselves, it is there by instinct. Paul, the apostle, speaks of the way that he is constantly reaching out towards this when he says, 'Not that I have already attained all this, or have already been made perfect, but I press on to take hold of that for which Christ took hold of me.'[4]

There's a distress and a thrill which run side by side over this whole matter. The distress is that however hard we try we don't match up to what we desire to be. We know what the standard is but we simply cannot achieve it. The experience of all of humanity has been the same, when we are confronted by the holiness of God. Whilst we worship it, we also kneel before it and cry, 'Woe is me!' Whilst he is worthy, we are unworthy. Whilst he is perfection, we are corrupted. Whilst he is flawless, we are blemished. Whilst he is pure, we are sinful. However, that is precisely the humbling that we need to drive us to Christ, for it is only in him and through him that we can receive the cleansing that we need. There is only one place where our sinfulness can be dealt with completely and that is at the cross of Calvary. The place where the one with the face that shines like the sun has died for us.

---

[4] Philippians 3:12.

Because of that cross there is also a thrill here as we contemplate the sunshine-faced Jesus. For as the cross of Jesus has dealt with our past so the Spirit of Jesus applies the value of that cross as he is actively at work within us dealing with our present and our future. The extraordinary anticipation which is the hope of every Christian is that 'when Jesus appears, we shall be like him.'[5] This is almost beyond our imagination. Not only will everyone and everything around us be perfect, but we too will be perfect like Jesus is perfect. Don't we desire that with all our hearts? To see the back of failure, of uncontrolled appetites, of an ill-disciplined mind, of soiled aspirations, very simply to see the back of our fallenness? It isn't just anticipated, it is guaranteed. 'The righteous will shine like the sun in the kingdom of their Father.'[6]

Thinking moment

- God is being worshipped in heaven for his holiness. How does the holiness of God fit in with his other characteristics like love, compassion, mercy and justice?

- Do you long to be holy as the Lord is holy? Do you find that an attractive prospect? What progress are you making in personal holiness?

- Do you have the hope that when you see Jesus you will be like him? What emotion does that create in you?

---

[5] 1 John 3:2.
[6] Matthew 13:43.

Chapter 10

A drop-dead moment (Revelation 1:17-20)

'When I saw him, I fell at his feet as though dead. Then he placed his right hand on me and said: "Do not be afraid. I am the First and the Last. I am the Living One; I was dead, and now look, I am alive for ever and ever! And I hold the keys of death and Hades. "Write, therefore, what you have seen, what is now and what will take place later"' (Revelation 1:17-19)

Seven seconds to make a first impression on another human being? This vision of Jesus must have lasted for much more than that, but short or long, it was enough for certain aspects of the vision to bite into John's memory and he was able to record them for us afterwards. John goes on to tell us of the impact of what he had seen.

His initial response was one of involuntary prostration. 'When I saw him, I fell at his feet as though dead', said John.[1] He didn't ask himself, what shall I do? The vision of Jesus was like a scythe which cut his legs from under him. He didn't look around to see how others might be responding. His immediate reaction is prostration before the Lord. Everything these days is described as 'unprecedented' but John's response to the glory of Jesus in this vision is not unprecedented; rather, it is typical of the response of believers throughout the generations. Ezekiel in Old Testament times had similar visions of the glory of God and he just couldn't stay standing upright. Repeatedly he tells us that when he saw the glory of the Lord the immediate impact was that he 'fell face down', and this happened again and again on several different occasions.'[2]

---

[1] Revelation 1:17.
[2] Ezekiel 1:28; 3:23; 11:13; 43:3-4.

Not only was this the experience of others but it wasn't even unprecedented for John himself. When he was on Mount Hermon all those years earlier with Jesus, and Peter, and his brother James, as Jesus' face began to shine like the sun and his clothes became white as light and they heard the voice of God himself saying, 'This is my Beloved Son. Listen to him,' they all fell to the ground on their faces.[3] John saw Jesus in his naked glory on the mount of transfiguration, and here now he was seeing him again in exactly the same way on the island of Patmos. By this point John was in his nineties. He had lived physically with Jesus for three years, non-stop. He had seen Jesus after his resurrection on numerous occasions. He had walked as a disciple of the Lord over the decades into his old age, so he is no inexperienced newbie to the Christian faith but when he sees the naked glory of Jesus he's prostrate.

What does this say to us about the nature of worship? What does it say to us about the way that we should approach the Lord? What does it say to us about what lies ahead of us? The companionship of a glorious, glorious Jesus; awe-full, breathtaking, stunning, wonderful, spectacular, magnificent. What quality, what depths, what content our worship should have. What glory is here to be experienced and celebrated.

What John witnessed in his vision was inspiring, thrilling, and exciting but it was also terrifying and frightening, so much so that it took his legs from under him. It was a mixture of both thrill and fear. Here lies an important spiritual principle. We are to fear the Lord but we are not to be frightened of him. There is an immense difference between the two. I know a man who frightens me a great deal. He always comes up with some unpredictable criticism, and he needles me every time we meet. I avoid his company because of it. But there is another man who is far ahead of me in learning and Biblical knowledge and godly grace. I fear him,

---

[3] Matthew 17:6.

because I don't match up to him but I love his company despite the fact that he shows up my weaknesses so clearly. We are to fear the Lord and long for his company rather than to be terrified of him and stay as far away as we can. Because this is true, the first thing that the Lord did when John was face down on the floor was to touch him. John says, that 'he placed his right hand on me.'[4]

Jesus didn't shake him to get him to come to his senses, or in order to wake him up. There is no criticism or rebuke here as he takes him by the shoulder. There's no implied disapproval, questioning him as to why he's down on the ground. Rather, it's a comforting touch of reassurance. And once again for John it is not unprecedented, for precisely the same thing happened on the mount of transfiguration. John and the other disciples were face down on the ground and Jesus came to them and touched them. John had felt this touch before. The decades fall away as he feels the Lord's hand upon him and he's back in that sacred place once again with his Lord.

How people longed for the touch of Jesus. They wanted it for their children, that they might be blessed and enjoy the favour of God in their growing years.[5] The blind, the deaf, the diseased, the distressed, the deformed, the broken, the grieving, the hopeless, the comfort-less, they cried out for his touch; they came close so that they could experience his touch and it was always powerful, healing and restorative.[6]

Having got John to his feet, the Lord then pours reassuring truth into his mind and soul. Jesus boxes him in with four-sided truth. Truth which lifts, invigorates, stimulates and energizes when it is believed and enjoyed.

---

[4] Revelation 1:17.
[5] Matthew 19:13-14.
[6] Matthew 8:3; 8:15; 9:29; 20:34.

Firstly, the Lord begins by reminding John who he is. 'I am' is the beginning of his next sentence.[7] This is God's shorthand name for himself. 'I am who I am.'[8] Who is John seeing? The 'I am'. Who is touching him? The 'I am'. Who is talking with him? The 'I am'. What are his problems at the moment? Exile, loneliness, separation from his friends and family. 'I am.' Comfort, companionship, care, compassion, gentleness and concern are in the heart of the Jesus who was speaking with him then and he is still the same now, today. John is so safe. The troubles which are on his mind take on a new proportion and perhaps they melt away in the presence of the 'I am.'

But there's more, secondly, for Jesus said, 'I am the first and the last.'[9] As we face the complexities of our national, political, social, cultural life; as we find ourselves over-whelmed by the problems and all around us are searching for solutions; as we ask the question, 'How on earth did we get here?', back comes the reply from heaven, 'I am the first.' 'Before Abraham was born, 'I am.'[10] It's okay. The Lord was there at the beginning and he has been overseeing everything since the beginning. But then we ask, 'Where will it all end?' and back comes the reply, 'I am the last.'[11] Where is history going? All in his direction. We only need to read the rest of this revelation and we will see how it's going to finish. It doesn't look hopeful in many ways, in so many of our circumstances, in the lives of our children, in the school, at work, in our marriage, in politics, between nations but Jesus confidently proclaims, 'I am the first and the last.'

Yet that is not all, for Jesus goes on to erect a third side to the box which will enclose John and hem him in with spiritual truth, 'I was

---

[7] Revelation 1:17.
[8] Exodus 3:14.
[9] Revelation 1:17.
[10] John 8:58.
[11] Revelation 1:17.

dead and behold I'm alive for ever and ever,'[12] says Jesus. The early Christians were completely obsessed with the resurrection of Jesus, and it is so unfortunate that we are not. They seemed to talk of nothing else. They couldn't get over the resurrection. It is hardly surprising considering that the apostles had witnessed the crucifixion and death of Jesus. They had witnessed or were aware of the rock-hewn tomb where he had been buried. Some of them had visited it and discovered that it was empty on Easter Sunday morning and then over the following weeks they had spoken to and kept company with the resurrected Jesus in all kinds of unexpected and unpredictable circumstances.

When we listen to someone preaching the Gospel today we don't think that they have done it faithfully unless they have spoken about the cross. In the early church they didn't think that someone had faithfully preached the Gospel unless they had spoken about the resurrection. 'With great power the apostles continued to testify to the resurrection and much grace was upon them all.'[13] This was the constant theme of their proclamation, for several good reasons. Firstly, it established clearly in the minds of everyone that Jesus was who he claimed to be. If he was a fraud or a charlatan then God the Father would have been glad to see him dead and buried, and for that to be the end of him. But by raising him from the dead the Father declared to all that Jesus is his Son.[14]

But the second reason they talked so much about the resurrection was because the truth of what happened on that Easter morning raises our expectations. It reminds us that the impossible is possible and we pray with greater faith and expectation as a result. We live more hopefully of the intervention of the Lord. We are more open to it and expectant of it. A focus on the resurrection emphasises Jesus' availability. This was not a once a year

---

[12] Revelation 1:18.
[13] Acts 4:33.
[14] Romans 1:3-4.

celebration for the early church but a continual daily reality. As a result they saw more miraculous things happening than we could dream of. 'I am alive for ever and ever.'

As if that was not sufficient for John, Jesus closes his box of security and hope with a fourth side when he said, 'I hold the keys of death and Hades.'[15] Hades is the place of departed spirits. It's where Jesus went whilst his body was still in the tomb. At the point of death there is a separation between the spirit and the body. The body remains here and gradually decays. For the Christian, the spirit leaves the body and is immediately secure in the presence of the Lord. Hades is not Gehenna which is the place of torment, but it is the place of the spirits of the dead. Jesus holds the keys to death and Hades and as a result he is able to guarantee our destiny beyond the grave as we head towards our own resurrection, our new heavenly body and the certainty of eternity with him.

Our experience of life tells us that death is a door that only opens one way. It has a sign over the top of the doorway which says 'Exit only.' We see people going through it but never coming back again. They go through it and we never see them again. But Jesus says to John, 'I've got the key to that door.' In fact, John knows that he has the keys to that door because he has seen Jesus go both ways. He saw Jesus die, leave, and be buried. But then he also saw him raised, coming from the grave. He was one of those early witnesses to see an empty tomb with only the grave clothes in which Jesus was buried remaining on the hard stone ledge of the burial chamber. He saw that.

Jesus is the only man who has ever been able to turn the exit door from this world into a swing door and as a result he encourages us to grieve with hope.[16] The non-Christian world around us can only look backwards during a funeral whilst the Christian always looks

---

[15] Revelation 1:18.
[16] 1 Thessalonians 4:13.

forward as well.   A friend who has recently received two life threatening diagnoses one after the other, with either one of them enough to bring on a depression confidently stated, 'But I have a future.'

On one occasion I was told by a member of my congregation never to use again a reference I had made to Bishop Cuthbert Bardsley. He was Bishop of Coventry in the 1970s. The story is told of Bishop Cuthbert visiting a teenager who was terminally ill, and he stood by his bedside and said, 'I hear you are going to die. How absolutely thrilling.'[17]   That is the Christian hope and those who have grasped the fact that Jesus is the Living One will share that confidence.

Jesus promised that he would take those who believe in him to be with him where he is.[18] He said that he was going to prepare a place for them there. But our Christian hope is greater still even than that, because Jesus will give us a new resurrection body just like his own.   He promises four times, almost without taking breath, that he will raise us up on the last day.[19]

Paul elaborates still further on this theme and describes in greater detail what we are to expect. He says

> So will it be with the resurrection of the dead. The body that is sown is perishable, it is raised imperishable; it is sown in dishonour, it is raised in glory; it is sown in weakness, it is raised in power; it is sown a natural body, it is raised a spiritual body. If there is a natural body, there is also a spiritual body.[20]

---

[17] Donald Coggan, *Cuthbert Bardsley: bishop, evangelist, pastor* (Glasgow: Collins, 1989) p.200.
[18] John 14:1-4.
[19] John 6:39,40,44,54.
[20] 1 Corinthians 15:42-44.

Key-holders are important people. They have to be trustworthy, reliable, honourable and responsible. Keys are only entrusted to those who have proved their ability in the past. That is why Jesus is the key-holder of the gate of death and Hades. He has passed through it both ways.

But this comforting and reassuring vision is not just for John. As so often when the Lord is at work in our lives, he wants the blessings that he gives to us to work for the benefit of others, too. We are to comfort others with the comfort that we ourselves have received from the Lord. As we have been reassured and strengthened by a variety of Biblical truths, we are to share them with others so that they can be encouraged and strengthened too.[21] So this vision and the truths which it contained are to be written down for seven churches in Asia Minor but also to be written down for the benefit of the church in succeeding generations. 'John, I want you to write a book.'[22]

The Lord is not going to dictate it word for word, apart from the letters to the seven churches, but after that he will show John a series of visions or revelations and he leaves it to John to describe them and write them down. So in a very real way, the Lord is the author of the book and John is the scribe. By this stage in his life, he has already written his Gospel biography of Jesus. He also would have written three letters which are included in the Bible but now almost at the end of his life, he is to record two more things. He is to write 'what is now and what will take place later.'[23]

This vision of Jesus is for all Christians for all time. The way that Jesus appears in the vision is the way that Jesus is. That's a permanent encouragement to us and will help us to navigate our daily lives with greater confidence and success. If we can grasp

---

[21] 2 Corinthians 1:4
[22] Revelation 1:11, 19.
[23] Revelation 1:19.

clearly what is to take place later, then that too will strengthen our resolve, give us confidence in the face of uncertainties and hope in the face of reverses. For the plans of God are progressing towards a climax. In that climax, evil will be destroyed in its entirety once and for all. Also in that climax, there will be the complete victory of all things good, godly, righteous, and holy.

So here is a man in his nineties with a writing commission to put on paper for the whole church to be able to read what God's plan for this planet is, and what his plans for his people are. What could be better than that for John, and what could be better than that for us?

Thinking moment

- Have you felt the power of Jesus' touch in your life in the past? Do you need to feel it afresh today for some reason? If so, ask!

- Paul the apostle wrote that 'for me to live is Christ and to die is gain.'[24] Can you echo those sentiments?

- 'I have a future', is a strong Christian statement of confidence in what lies beyond the grave for every believer. Is this a confidence which you share? Where do our certainties lie as those who are disciples of Jesus?

---

[24] Philippians 1:21.

By the same author

Recovering His Reputation: the ministry of a late developer

What is really going on when a church grows? In a book which distils reflections on quarter of a century of ministry based in a growing church, Bishop Stuart Bell answers that question. His answer takes the reader on a journey of exploration, into strategies and plans, but still more into the spiritual heart of Christian leadership. These unfolding reflections bring us face to face with the disciplines and struggles, the joys and the challenges of walking with Jesus daily, in order to serve a church which aimed to 'Recover His Reputation'.

Available on Amazon in paperback and on Kindle.

'This remarkable book on leading a church draws upon Stuart Bell's many decades of proclaiming Christ with power and influence. Overflowing with honesty, wisdom and insight, it should be compulsory reading for all who are called to be shepherds of God's flock. Recommended without reservation!'
J. John – author and International Evangelist.

Printed in Great Britain
by Amazon

35472240R00050